From Beginning to End

FROM
BEGINNING
TO END

The Rituals of Our Lives

ROBERT
FULGHUM

PUBLISHED BY RANDOM HOUSE LARGE PRINT
IN ASSOCIATION WITH VILLARD BOOKS,
A DIVISION OF RANDOM HOUSE, INC.
NEW YORK 1995

*The Library of Congress has catalogued the
Villard edition as follows:*
Fulghum, Robert
From beginning to end: the rituals of our lives /
Robert Fulghum   p. cm.
Includes biographical references.
ISBN 0-679-41961-6
1. Conduct of life. 2. Rites and ceremonies—Miscellanea.
I. Title.   BJ1595.F85   1995   392—dc20   94-4407
Random House Large Print ISBN: 0-679-44339-8

MANUFACTURED IN THE UNITED STATES OF AMERICA
FIRST LARGE PRINT EDITION

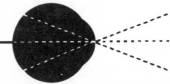

This Large Print Book carries the
Seal of Approval of N.A.V.H.

From beginning to end,
the rituals of our lives shape each hour,
day, and year.
Everyone leads a ritualized life:
Rituals are repeated patterns of meaningful acts.
If you are mindful of your actions, you will see
the ritual patterns.
If you see the patterns, you may understand them.
If you understand them, you may enrich them.
In this way, the habits of a lifetime become sacred.

Is this so?

If you and I had sat on a park bench for an afternoon a couple of years ago, catching up, talking of this and that, and you had asked me the "what-are-you-thinking-and-writing-about-these-days?" kind of question, I would have answered, "Rituals." And I would have added, "If that surprises you, it surprises me, as well."

Why "rituals"? It's a formal topic, most likely addressed by theologians and anthropologists. My interests are not usually so academic. The commonplace and daily aspects of life attract me most. And the anecdotal essay is my style of reporting what I notice.

So why "rituals"?

My thinking was set in motion by those who, knowing I was a parish minister for many years, have asked me for advice about ceremonies and celebrations. They wanted words to use at graduations, funerals, and the welcoming of children. They inquired about grace at family meals, the reaffirmation of wedding vows, and ways to heal wounds suffered in personal conflict. People requested help with the rituals of solitude, such as meditation, prayer, and contemplation.

I'm supposed to know about such things. But the truth is that while I've performed and participated in such rituals for many years, I've never given the subject the careful thought it deserves.

While seeking ways of responding to those requests, I began seeing much of my life and the life around me as ritualized. I realized that the important rituals were not stored in books and service manuals but were being lived daily by all of us.

If the topic of "rituals" were a building, its appearance would be imposingly serious—like the antique administration building of a small college. If you went into the main entrance and on into the foyer, the intimidating formality would continue.

If you asked at the main desk for information about the college, you'd receive the official brochures and handbooks that are idealized maps about the activities of an institution. That's one way to look at information and learning.

If, instead, you went around back, entered through the kitchen door of the cafeteria in the basement, and talked with the cooks and janitors, and then went on into the lunchroom to sit down and chat with the staff and students, you might feel more at ease, and would likely get a friendlier view of the college.

I prefer this informal, backstage view of life.

It is there I have looked for the raw materials out of which rituals are made.

Following my nose and intuition, I've found my-self in unexpected places thinking unanticipated thoughts. It's always gratifying to see something familiar in a new light, and to realize that what I am looking for is close by. It's like finding my "lost" glasses perched on the end of my nose. So has it been with this search for an understanding of rituals. Right there in front of my face all along.

If you and I ate lunch together regularly over a period of time, I'd tell you what I know now about rituals, expecting you would add what you know. And my guess is that you'd be as surprised as I was by how much you know about rituals, and by how much ritual behavior goes on in your life.

My confidence in the nature of our discussions comes from two experiences in the summer of 1994. After I had put my thinking about rituals on paper, I asked eighteen friends to read the manuscript while we were on a rafting trip together on the Rogue River in Oregon. Two weeks later, I took a revised manuscript to a summer family conference where 180 adults read it. On the river or in camp, the result was the same: intense and lengthy dialogue of the sort that keeps people talking way into the night about things that matter to them.

When we have this richness of contact with one another, we use the language of personal intimacy—the language of informal conversation rather than the formal language of the college lecture hall. We speak out of our own experience—from what we know firsthand—and illustrate our convictions with anecdotes out of our lives or the lives we observe. Such is the style of this book.

–

To follow these comments with the conventional form of a Table of Contents doesn't quite work. The summer river trip I mentioned suggests a solution. Each morning at breakfast we were given a preview of the day on the water. Our boatman had the uncanny ability to give us both enough information about the character of the day's stretch of river to relieve our anxiety and at the same time not to tell us so much that there was nothing left for us to discover on our own. He understood the need for the right mix of useful information and adventure.

Typically, he'd tell us there were three put-your-life-jackets-on rapids in the first two miles, some long and easy slack water when we could swim and have water fights or whatever, then a late lunch stop alongside a falls where boats had to be portaged, and then a long afternoon stretch of easy water broken up occasionally by riffles and "fun stuff"—surprises such as a rope swing or slimy mud or a side canyon.

Instead of a Table of Contents, then, here's information you may find useful—in the spirit of a boatman's view of the river.

Within

While the actual passages of life may follow in consequential order: birth, adolescence, marriage, retirement, and death, the actual lives we live are seldom so orderly. And we don't give consideration to these life events as they happen to us. Reflection comes later—when we observe what happens to someone else. You don't consider your own birth at birth, but later, when you have children or someone close to you does. You don't think about death much until you get real close to it, at a funeral perhaps, and that can happen at any time during your life. The ritual aspects of life might be considered in any order. Here's my approach—feel free to follow your own.

The rituals of the first hour of the day, as seen through a window in the life of one person. As the Holy is made out of the Daily, the Simple becomes Sacred.

The premises on which the discussion of rituals

depends, illustrated with anecdotes. The differences between ritual and rite of passage, and how these ideas affect the public, private, and secret levels of life.

A CEMETERY VIEW *page 29*

An answer to the question ''If you knew you had a limited amount of time to live, what would you do?''

ONCE *page 41*

Stories that come from asking people to continue this sentence: ''I never will forget the first time I . . .'' The ritual of remembering.

REUNION *page 59*

The rituals of returning and the rites of reconciliation—with people, things, experiences, and feelings—as pertaining to high school, family, adoption, communion, talismans, conventions, and God.

UNION *page 129*

The public observance of a wedding as a model of the ways in which all public rituals are observed and reformed. First, the actual wedding, then a backstage view of how the ceremony came about.

BORN *page 181*

A celebration of the welcoming of a child into a neighborhood and the welcoming of a neighborhood into the life of a child.

From Beginning to End

BEGINNING

*The seeds of the day are best
planted in the first hour.*

DUTCH PROVERB

My friend Alice seems to have arrived at the threshold of living one day at a time. It's calming to be in her unhurried, gentle presence. She used to be as manic and driven as anyone I knew. But not now. Something's different. She says it has to do with the way she begins her day. Her morning ritual. "I've got the first hour going pretty well; maybe the rest of the day will follow in time."

As is often the case, good news is not very dramatic. No sudden violence or crisis shaped what Alice does each day—she lived her way into it little by little. I share her story because it has health and sanity in it. In looking at rituals, I've tried to stay away from the illness models of life—away from what's wrong—and have sought the company and testimony of people whose lives seem to be working well. We're all too familiar with toxic habit patterns. Better to consider healthy models. It's like shifting from a focus on divorced couples to studying successful marriages. Everybody knows what can go wrong. My question is, "What can go right?"

Alice has an answer.

I'll deliberately leave what she looks like to your

imagination. You'll get enough information about her as we go along to bring her to life in your mind. You know someone like her already—you may even *be* someone like her.

One spring the women in Alice's office were passing around self-improvement books. About dieting, exercise, and spirituality. Creating a "you-could-do-better" atmosphere. Alice thought "could-do-better" was as often a curse as an encouragement. She thumbed through the books out of courtesy, not personal interest.

Though she couldn't remember exactly when the line was crossed from the restless discontent of her thirties to her present state of mind, she was, in her forties, reasonably content with her life. Maybe someday she would get back to "could-do-better," but she was now in a "this-will-do" phase of her life, and she found it unexpectedly satisfying.

Though she was not as thin, attractive, smart, healthy, or happy as she might have been, she was thin enough, attractive enough, smart enough, healthy enough, and happy enough. An outsider might see room for improvement, and some expert might show her ways in which further ambition might pay off in the long run. And she supposed that the urge for change would rise up again out of unforeseen circumstances. Still, it pleased her to realize for *the time being* it was a *just being* time. Life was fine, especially when she considered it one day at a time, and one morning at a time.

—

This understanding came to her one afternoon, riding the bus home from work. As she fell into that meditative trance-state bus travel induces, she thought about her life and realized her daily routine was composed of habits so carefully observed she might call them sacred—because she honored them as surely as if she had joined a religious order. They had become that important to her.

Some might think she was lonely—her son was away at college, her daughter working in Portland, and her husband, a field geologist, was gone a good deal of the time. She wasn't lonely, though. She realized she was accepting, even welcoming, of the unplanned solitude—especially the solitude after daybreak each day. This regular, reliable morning stillness had become a cherished part of her life.

She had often wondered exactly why the Lord's Prayer had the line in it "Give us this day our daily bread." Now, on these mornings in the middle years of her life, she thought she had it figured out. Perhaps it meant, "Let this day suffice—let it be."

—

Just before six A.M., she began waking—floating up out of the night world—aware that somehow her mind was alert, though her eyes were not open and her body wasn't moving. Though she hadn't needed an alarm clock in several years, she often set the timer in the stereo in the living room to play music at six. When the music began, she began to rise. Without conscious effort or intention, her eyes would open, and she would roll over, sit on the edge of the bed, and stand in one easy motion.

"Good morning, Alice," she greeted herself.

Determined not to begin the morning with a sense of urgency, she stretched and yawned and stood still, looking out the window. She didn't turn on the lights right away—the artificial light was too jarring—so she was content moving about in the soft half-light of daybreak, or else, in winter, with candlelight, putting on this new day as comfortably as she put on her robe.

Her robes were seasonal. She hadn't exactly planned it that way, but that's how it evolved. In winter there was a long, warm deep purple terry-cloth robe her mother gave her for Christmas. It was beginning to fade, but she liked the connection with her mother and her childhood. The robe, like her relationship with her mother, had softened with age.

In spring she changed to a new blue-and-white cotton kimono given to her by a Japanese exchange student she had befriended. It made her think of faraway places where she had never been.

In summer there was a white chenille bathrobe with a pattern on it that reminded her of the spread on her grandmother's bed. She found it at a neighborhood garage sale. Instant nostalgia. And she was childishly amused by the patterns it left on her skin when she lay down on the couch in it. It was the closest she would come to having tattoos.

And in the fall she wore a cotton robe her husband had brought her as a surprise gift from a business trip somewhere. Printed with flowers—mostly orange and yellow and red—like the colors of leaves in autumn. She wore this robe at other times, as well—when he was away and she missed him, and when he came home—to please him.

These robes were not part of some conscious fashion scheme—not purchased by her or acquired all at once. They had accumulated and been made important by use and association. She changed robes by some unconscious prompting from weather and daylight. They were useful, practical garments, but when she thought about it, she realized she wore them as much for the feelings and memories they evoked as for their physical comfort. When I told her I thought her robes had become like temple garments, she smiled and replied, ''Yes.''

The habits of her morning had acquired value in the same way as the robes. Only when she began taking notice of her morning routines did she realize how important these habits had become—how they were rituals of rightness and not just routine. The word ''sacred'' could be honestly applied. What had changed about her life was her becoming mindful of what already existed.

Going into the bathroom was always the first act of the new day. The toilet first, then the basin, where she washed her face, brushed her teeth, combed her hair—all the while considering herself in the mirror. Every day of her life she met herself in the mirror.

She had a habit of closing her eyes while she brushed her teeth—though she didn't know why—and it amused her. Even when she thought, I'm not going to close my eyes this time, she always did. She often thought about her "pilots"—the automatic one and the conscious one, and this teeth-brushing thing was like a contest between them. When she closed her eyes, she saw herself in her mind's mirror as a dutiful child, doing the right thing. The routine of brushing her teeth had become a habit associated with virtue. Teeth-brushing and rightness were inter-twined.

—

After the bathroom came the kitchen—flipping the switch to the coffee grinder and turning the fire on under the kettle on the stove. Nothing said "Good morning!" better than the smell of coffee. Then a glass of juice from the refrigerator. It seemed as if someone else had prepared this welcome to her in the kitchen each morning: the person she was yesterday. She liked having these things ready to go the night before. There was a certain comforting quality about it—it meant her life was in order.

From the kitchen, she moved out through the living room to open the front door, consider the day, check the weather and the season. She thought of this as getting the early-morning news of the world. Rain, sun, spring, snow—wind or calm—there was always this local news to consider.

Picking up the paper from the front steps, she un- wrapped it as she walked back through the house into the kitchen to brew the coffee. She had mixed feel- ings about reading the newspaper. So much of its contents dealt with death and disease and crime and violence everywhere in the world. She cared—cared to the point of despair sometimes—but it was hard to begin the day with this news. Sometimes she put the front section of the paper away to face in the evening and turned to the less disturbing parts.

She always looked at the ''Peanuts'' cartoon strip and the weather map.

And she usually checked her horoscope. Not that she really believed in astrology, but she was fas- cinated by the writer's skill in making such clever predictions that could be interpreted to fit so many individual situations. She realized that she was doing what people had been doing for thousands of years— consulting oracles, throwing the bones, checking with the fates.

And then there were those days when her horo- scope was absolutely right-on. That amazed and baf- fled her—gave her one more connection with the many mysteries she recognized as part of being alive. The mysteries didn't diminish with age—the older she got, the more mystery she encountered. Someday there would be nothing left but mystery.

By mystery she also meant those things she understood but could not speak of for lack of adequate
words. Maybe death was like that—the place where
mystery and understanding finally became one.

Some days she ignored the paper altogether. And
she never turned on the television in the morning.
Mornings were best when she was alone in her mind
and had no interference with her mood and thinking.
Often she took her coffee into the living room and sat
in a chair by the window, listening to music, looking
out at the day and the world. She supposed this was
what people meant by meditation. Perhaps it was her
form of morning prayer.

Next she set out cereal and fruit for herself, and
poured dry food into the dog's bowl. Opening the
back door, she was greeted by the enthusiasm of the
old dog, barking, licking, jumping, wagging, wig-
gling in his arthritic way. "Good morning, Elvis."
She thought he looked rather like Elvis Presley,
hence the name. And it amused her to think that Elvis
was alive and reasonably well in her backyard.

In summertime she took her food and his food outside, and they sat together and had breakfast. She had
never been particularly crazy about dogs, but this
stray had showed up in her yard one day, clearly in
need of food and attention, looking like Elvis in his
last days, and so—well, one thing had led to another.

They were deeply attached now. Most relationships happened like that, or so it seemed to her. Circumstances, luck, mutual need, affection, and time played a part. No relationships were made in heaven. They were made because living things were looking for good company. And when you found good company, you valued it deeply and were responsible for its upkeep and well-being.

So now she had a dog. And the dog also had her. He was an aged, independent dog who could mind his own business or give her attention, and he seemed to know when to do which. She felt he was wiser and more experienced in the ways of the world than she. Elvis had been around. And it was good to have his protection at night, his company in the morning, and the knowledge that whenever she came home, she would be enthusiastically welcomed in the most straightforward, uncomplicated way.

–

While she dressed for work, there was always a short time when she was nude in front of the mirror. Daily, she examined her breasts for any signs of abnormality—cancer was a real and serious fear. Her mom had breast cancer. And barely survived the treatment. Alice knew the daily check was obsessive, but deep down she was afraid. She knew no matter how well your life is going, death is always around somewhere—she couldn't pretend she didn't think about it. And though a realist about the possibility of cancer, she approached this regular examination as another spiritual exercise. She tried to balance the fear in her mind with her belief that she had the power to help her body maintain its health.

At the same time, she always appraised the rest of her body, seeing the slight-but-sure downhill droop of things. The law of gravity is never repealed. She had always admired older women who accepted aging sufficiently to continue wearing bathing suits and going swimming long after their bodies had passed the model body stage. She felt accepting one's body was important to accepting one's soul. This wasn't all that easy to do sometimes, but she thought of it as a spiritual exercise, not a matter of fashion.

This morning routine and the attention she paid to it had taken on the quality of the first service of the day in her personal religious order. And it had come about naturally as she found her way toward inner peace in her middle years. It was as if the center of her life had shifted away from outward concerns for family and work to the interior condition of the life itself.

When she reflected on how mornings had been when her children were small, she saw that those days, too, had their sacred habits. There was just less time to think about it then. Now she remembered. Being wakened by little warm, sleepy bodies crawling under the covers. Bathing and dressing and singing and talking with a child each morning, making lunches, and the short calm period of relief mixed with anxiety and regret as a child was bid good-bye and sent out the door to school. Part of her morning ritual now was this ritual of remembering the mornings of the past.

When her husband was home during the week, his morning routine was similar to hers. Probably for the same reasons. They seldom talked in the morning. Not because they didn't have anything to say, but because they didn't have to say anything. They were in touch, but not with words.

Recently, though, they had been talking about observing the Sabbath. When the children were young, they had all gone to church on Sunday mornings and used the rest of the day to catch up with all the busywork of running a household. When the kids grew up, they had stopped regular churchgoing, and Sundays became even busier with mundane tasks. Saturday and Sunday blended into one frantic blur. Errands, house repairs, bill paying, social obligations—busywork that left them tired and grumpy in bed by the end of Sunday evenings. Sometimes they fought.

But now they were working at observing the Sabbath. This was a conscious effort—something they had sorted out together over breakfast last winter. It wasn't always easy or even possible to keep the Sabbath. But it was something they both wanted. And needed.

The common rule was to have a day disconnected

from work, obligations, and incoming complications. To not have to do anything or go anywhere. They stopped taking the Sunday paper and didn't listen to the radio or watch television. Arising late, they spent time together—making waffles in midmorning, going for walks, reading books, listening to music—perhaps going to a movie in the late afternoon on rainy Sundays.

Every day couldn't be like this, but Alice would settle for good mornings and at least one day a week lived ''one day at a time.''

When the Sabbath day worked, the best part was just sitting still together—just she and her husband—like being in a private church in a way, but in their bathrobes on the back steps in summer, not in a pew. She knew now that this ritual was religious—not in the usual, obvious, conventional ways. But religious ritual, nonetheless.

Sometimes it was all the quiet joy she could bear—and tears came to her eyes. She sat still, noticing the world, feeling her husband's nearness, being at home in her skin as well as in the universe, drinking the first cup of coffee in the quiet, dignified company of old Elvis, slowly thumping his crooked tail.

By the living-room fire in winter—in the backyard in summer.

Just being there was enough.

If she had a tail, she would have joined in the thumping.

∾

If we called in an anthropologist now and asked her to examine this account of Alice's morning and Sabbath routines, I submit she would see ritual behavior of the most classic kind—the kind that gives structure and meaning to daily life. Behavior that is regularly repeated because it serves a profound purpose.

If we called in a theologian for a similar consideration, my bet is the presence of the bedrock of religion would be affirmed—a deep sense of connection through action with the unnameable wonder and mystery of life.

Getting a little distance from one's behavior can be enlightening.

When Alice became mindful of what she had somewhat unconsciously constructed for herself, she used the language of ritual and religion to speak of her morning and acknowledged that the deep desire planted in her soul for being at home in her own skin and her world had slowly but surely flowered. She also felt these mornings were a threshold—a passageway—into her next stage of life.

PROPOSITIONS

All things which make noise at the side of the path do not come down the path.

AFRICAN PROVERB

Midway in my inquiry into rituals, I summarized my thinking into some working hypotheses I call "propositions." The fourteen simple statements on this list are tentative conclusions, which is why they are followed by a question: Is this so? I mean the propositions to function as a kind of magnifying glass used to examine all the examples of ritual behavior I've encountered.

That process gave this book its structure: considerations followed by stories and anecdotes followed by reflections and conclusions, and back to stories once more. We're still in the spirit of lunchtime conversation. It's as if I've gone home and thought about the stories told yesterday and have returned to share the reflective sorting out that went on in my mind since last we talked.

The propositions:

· To be human is to be religious.
· To be religious is to be mindful.
· To be mindful is to pay attention.
· To pay attention is to sanctify existence.

· Rituals are one way in which attention is paid.
· Rituals arise from the stages and ages of life.
· Rituals transform the ordinary into the holy.

· Rituals may be public, private, or secret.
· Rituals may be spontaneous or arranged.
· Rituals are in constant evolution and reformation.

· Rituals create sacred time.
· Sacred time is the dwelling place of the Eternal.
· Haste and ambition are the adversaries
  of sacred time.

Is this so?

To be human is to be religious.

Every human being asks the elemental religious questions: Who am I? What am I doing here? Where did I come from before birth and what happens after I die? What's right and wrong and how do I know? What is the meaning of life, and how do I give meaning to my life? How do I account for the awesome, mysterious majesty of the universe, and what's my place in the scheme of things?

These questions are not provided by society or the church—they first rise out of the deep inner space of each person. And it has been so since the beginning of human consciousness.

To be religious is to be mindful.

When careful attention is given to these human questions, we find answers and hold to those answers with faith and devotion, thereby making them sacred to us. The asking and answering process itself sanctifies existence, and we repeat the process lifelong. Ritual is one name we give this repetition.

Our lives are endless ritual.

Patterns of repetition govern each day, week, year, and lifetime. "Personal habits" is one term we use to describe the most common of these repeated patterns. But I say these habits are sacred because they give deliberate structure to our lives. Structure gives us a sense of security. And that sense of security is the ground of meaning.

Rituals flow *from* the life of the individual *into* the church.

The rituals of the church are the organized, communal form of the needs and patterns of the life of the individual. Communal activity is one more way of supporting meaningful structure in the life of an individual.

The ritual moments of life mark changes from moment to moment, day to day, year to year, and from one stage of being to another. The conscious acknowledgments of these changes are called rites of passage. Sometimes we celebrate in public, sometimes in private, and most often, in secret. Sometimes we are aware of the importance of the moment and at other times its importance is established later, through the ritual of remembering. Consider the levels of rituals:

Public:

A wedding service is a rite of passage. A formal, *public* acknowledgment of the transition from single to married life. The Christian church has defined such a public event as a sacrament—an outward sign of an inner sacred circumstance.

There is a civil dimension to these rites, as well.

Official civil documents usually record these rites of passage: birth certificate, diploma, driver's license, draft card, voter-registration card, marriage license, deeds of ownership, will, and a death certificate.

Private:

On a *private* level, among family and friends, we celebrate birthdays, anniversaries, team membership and accomplishments, engagements, moving into a new home, and even clothes and equipment that signify change of status—high heels or shaving gear. The documents of these occasions are cards and letters, wrapping-paper remains, and dried flowers.

Secret:

There are passages in one's personal, solitary, *secret* life that are no less momentous. Puberty and adolescence are filled with such occasions—all those times when you alone know that some irrevocable alteration has come to your existence. The celebration comes in solitude, with no tangible evidence of change of status.

–

Public, private, and secret levels of ritual often intertwine. Many of the moments of secret passage preview the private and public rites of passage.

In the spring of my twelfth year, my mother thought I was finally old enough to be trusted to go downtown and back on the bus alone. She didn't know I was already way beyond buses. I had been driving her car around the neighborhood when she was away from home.

The rite of passage was in that scary moment—the first time I started the car, shifted into gear, and rolled off down the street thinking: *I am going to die.* And: *She is going to kill me.* And: *Ohmygod I'm driving!*

I went around the block only once. But that was enough. When I had safely parked the car in the driveway, I sat very still in the driver's seat, holding on to the wheel for a long time. A scared kid got into the car when this adventure began. When the door opened next, a *driver* got out—one who was driven to go on to whatever came next in the passages of autonomy.

I had passed over from one stage of life to another.

From child in danger to dangerous child.

When my father finally got around to teaching me to drive, he was impressed at my "natural" talent for driving. When I took my test and got my license and my father gave me my own set of keys to the car one night at dinner, it was a major rite of passage for him and my mother. Their perception of me had changed and was formally acknowledged. For me the occasion meant a *private* sanction to do in *public* what I had already been doing in *secret.*

The private family passage into a public status had been presaged by that secret first drive of terror and joy. No parent can provide that moment, and no civil authority can license it; but nothing can match it in one's memory. The shift of self-perception is the most powerful ingredient in the chain reaction of becoming the person you are always becoming.

—

Not unlike the event of being given the keys to the car was the man-to-man lecture my father gave me the summer of my twenty-first year. A week before I was to marry, he sat me down to explain sexual intercourse and gave me a box of condoms.

Little did he know.

Or maybe he did.

Only now do I begin to understand. My adult sons tell me what they knew about sex long before I realized their knowledge. And they tell me what they did behind my back when they were kids. I'm not surprised, actually. Because they knew what I knew and did what I did. And if my father were around to join this conversation, I'm quite sure he would chime in with descriptions of his own rites of passage not unlike ours. Only now, in the middle years of my life, do I understand this. *His life was like my life.*

And the patterns of his life—his rituals—and the patterns of his father's and his father's and his father's are like the ritual patterns of my sons and daughters and their sons and daughters and on and on and on.

It's not that I really needed to know about condoms and sex, and my father probably knew that. But I did need for my father to say, in his own way, "I see and affirm that you have become a man." And I wonder when his father did that for him and wonder if I have done that for my sons, as well.

This is the ritual dance between parents and children. We are always both ahead of and way behind one another in our rites of passage. Everything we do in our growing up has been done before. But it needs recognition and validation each time for each one of us—public, private, and secret. *The rituals must be observed.* The rituals are cairns marking the path behind us and ahead of us. Without them we lose our way.

∽

As these anecdotes illustrate, ritual refers to two kinds of acts: those things we do for the first time that, in fact, have been done by the human race again and again forever—and those patterns that we ourselves repeat again and again because they bring structure and meaning to our individual and collective lives.

A consideration of human and personal history will remind us that rituals are not set in concrete—that public forms, private celebrations, and even secret acts get modified over time to more nearly satisfy changing needs. This re-formation comes when we choose or are forced to consider the patterns of our lives.

I shall tell you of such a time of reconsideration.

But first, I'll show you a photograph.

A
CEMETERY
VIEW

*The art of living well and dying well
are one.*

EPICURUS

A caption for this photograph: *A man sitting in a chair in a cemetery, as a light rain fell and the sun shone at the same time, on the fourth day of June in 1994.*

If you were there, standing close by, you would notice that the sod beneath his chair was laid down in small square sections, suggesting it had been removed and then carefully replaced.

The man owns the property upon which he sits. He has paid for the site, paid to have the ground dug up, to have a cement vault installed, and to have the ground restored.

He is sitting on his own grave. Not because his death is imminent—he's in pretty good shape, actually. And not because he was in a morbid state of mind—he was in a fine mood when the picture was taken. In fact, he has had one of the most affirmative afternoons of his life.

Sitting for an afternoon on his own grave, he has had one of those potent experiences when the large pattern of his life has been unexpectedly reviewed: the past, birth, childhood, adolescence, marriage, career, the present, and the future. He has confronted finitude—the limits of life. The fact of his own death lies before him and beneath him—raising the questions of the when and the where and the how of it. What shall he do with his life between now and then?

—

I tell you these things with such certainty because the man is me. I speak of him in third person because I often think of him in third person.

He's the man in the bathroom mirror I see every day. For as long as I can remember, I have gone to meet him each morning. And I see him each night before I go to bed. Sometimes I ask myself: Who is he? What will become of him? This daily consideration of the reflection of the man in the mirror is the oldest ritual of my life. A sacred habit.

I recall when he was a kid going through puberty. I anxiously checked to see if he was becoming taller, growing hair, and getting pimples. I felt older than the kid in the mirror. Now I notice he's going through middle age, and I worry when I see he is growing wider, losing hair, and getting wrinkles. That man in the mirror is older than I am now. While I've been thirty for many years, he'll be fifty-eight next June.

I see his white hair and beard, the lines in his face, the liver spots and scars on his hands, the sagging of his flesh. And I wonder how far from making use of his gravesite he might be? He certainly looks closer to death than I am.

—

I've spent more time around death than most people. Thirty-four years as a minister: responding to late-night calls to come to the bedsides of the dying, comforting those who grieve and mourn, and officiating at well over a hundred funerals and memorial services. Death and I have been professional colleagues for most of my adult life.

Still, there has always been a distance between my thoughts about my own death and what I was called upon to do about the deaths of others. After all, I was a "professional." I can empathize with the funeral director who said to me, "I make the mistake of thinking death happens to other people, but not undertakers."

As I have become more aware of the aging of the man in the mirror, I realize he needs to attend to some necessary business—to do what I have often encouraged others to do: update his will, write out his funeral instructions, and fill out the necessary forms clarifying decisions with the People's Memorial Society to which he belongs. A practical tidying-up. And an existential clarification of the place of death in his life. The writing of this book provided a timely provocation to put his house in order.

My family was a little surprised when I broached the subject. They didn't realize how much thought I had been giving to death. They also respected the reasonableness of what I was doing. All of us know we should do this, but most of us just don't get around to it. Our survivors have to sort it out, and thereby we leave confusing decisions if not painful problems as our immediate legacy.

—

The first question: What was to become of the body of the man in the mirror when he dies? My family and I agreed on cremation, but they weren't comfortable with the scattering of ashes. The burial solution was close by. The Lake View Cemetery on Capitol Hill in Seattle has already been part of my life for many years. It's on my route when I go for early-morning walks, and I've officiated at burials there several times. The oldest cemetery in Seattle, it's quiet, peaceful, and unpretentious. I like the diversity of its population—names on tombstones suggest the occupants' roots are Chinese, Russian, Greek, French, Japanese, German, English, Norwegian, Italian, and more—an amazing mix of the immigrant stock from which this city has grown. I used to take my art history students there to see the remnant influence of the burial monuments of the Egyptians, Greeks, Romans, and ancient Chinese. Obelisks, columns, arches, and urns. The cemetery is small in acreage, but it's deep and wide in my imagination.

I like being there alive.

It's a good place to be dead.

—

So I made arrangements to select and purchase a plot. What an odd shopping experience. The rule of thumb in real estate decisions is "location, location, location." But for a grave, what difference does a view really make? Does it matter to me who my nearest neighbors are? And resale value is not really a concern, is it?

Still undecided, I asked my children to help me make the decision. They have to live with it, not me. Our discussion was awkward. Like something out of the story of "Goldilocks and the Three Bears."

"No, this one's too—well—public. No, this one's depressingly damp and moldy and down in a ravine—not a good place to come in winter. How about this one by the tree? Or this one by the funny tombstone. Or how about down by the Greeks—you like Greeks."

In *It Was on Fire When I Lay Down on It,* I wrote about the special respect I have for a bench marking a grave in this same cemetery. A bench indicating that someone went out of the way to think about the living who come here and wanted to say to them, in effect, "Sit down—make yourself comfortable." The words carved into the edge of the bench call your attention east to the mountains, west to the sea, north to the university, and to a magnificent dawn redwood tree close by to the south. It's an inspiring place to sit. Just twenty feet from that bench was an empty plot. Of course. Right there.

Once we agreed on the site, the cemetery workmen had to dig the grave before it could be sold to me. Because this is an old cemetery, and records were not always well kept, they had to be sure the site had no unrecorded occupant.

I came to the cemetery the day the workmen were digging my grave.

Now, I had stood beside empty graves before. But never beside my own. I was stunned by the experience. For days I couldn't get the image out of my mind. Not only was the man in the mirror going to be buried there. I was.

So, on New Year's Day of 1994, I took a folding chair up to the gravesite and sat down to think. And thought about the next twenty-one years.

Why twenty-one? I had asked a life-insurance agent to find out what my life expectancy was as of my next birthday. After a few questions about family and personal health and habits, he gave me twenty-one years. He would literally bet money on it—sell me an insurance policy.

Sure, anything can happen. But just suppose, for the sake of discussion, I knew for sure that the actuarial tables were accurate and I could count on those twenty-one years? What difference would it make?

As a minister, I am familiar with the thinking that people do when they are suddenly given six months to live by a doctor. And I'm familiar with similar life occasions when the recognition of your finitude suddenly brings you to some high place where your life is spread out before you: major surgery or a terrible accident, the death of a close friend or family member, the breakup of a family through divorce, recovery from alcoholism. Getting fired in midcareer, an emotional breakdown and recovery, and a major high school or college or family reunion are other such promptings. The ordinary flow of life stops, and you see your existence as a whole. You make some decisions about what gives it meaning and what takes away from a meaningful existence.

Success and failure come to mind.

And you are likely to notice patterns, seasons, and transitions.

Both in your life and in the lives of others.

It's useful to know that people have been deliberating just as you are for a long, long, long time. The most familiar expression of this awareness of the big picture was written more than two thousand years ago. We don't really know much about who wrote it or why. It's in what is often called the most puzzling book in the Bible. It's a succinct summary statement often used at weddings, birth celebrations, and funerals. It turns up in greeting cards, and I've even seen it on coffee mugs and T-shirts. Still, nothing diminishes its elegant declaration of truth. You may know parts of it by heart.

In Hebrew, to remind you of its age, it looks like this:

‎3 יְלַכֹּל זְמָן וְעֵת לְכָל־חֵפֶץ תַּחַת הַשָּׁמָיִם׃ ס

‎2 עֵת לָלֶדֶת וְעֵת לָמוּת
עֵת לָטַעַת וְעֵת לַעֲקוֹר נָטוּעַ׃

‎3 עֵת לַהֲרוֹג וְעֵת לִרְפּוֹא
עֵת לִפְרוֹץ וְעֵת לִבְנוֹת׃

‎4 עֵת לִבְכּוֹת וְעֵת לִשְׂחוֹק
עֵת סְפוֹד וְעֵת רְקוֹד׃

‎5 עֵת לְהַשְׁלִיךְ אֲבָנִים וְעֵת כְּנוֹס אֲבָנִים
עֵת לַחֲבוֹק וְעֵת לִרְחֹק מֵחַבֵּק׃

‎6 עֵת לְבַקֵּשׁ וְעֵת לְאַבֵּד
עֵת לִשְׁמוֹר וְעֵת לְהַשְׁלִיךְ׃

‎7 עֵת לִקְרוֹעַ וְעֵת לִתְפּוֹר
עֵת לַחֲשׁוֹת וְעֵת לְדַבֵּר׃

‎8 עֵת לֶאֱהֹב וְעֵת לִשְׂנֹא
עֵת מִלְחָמָה וְעֵת שָׁלוֹם׃ ס

Translated into modern English, Ecclesiastes 3:1–8 reads:

For everything there is a season,
And a time and purpose for every matter under
    heaven:
  a time to be born, and a time to die;
  a time to plant, and a time to pluck up what is
    planted;
  a time to kill, and a time to heal;
  a time to weep, and a time to laugh;
  a time to mourn, and a time to dance;
  a time to throw away stones, and a time to gather
    stones together;
  a time to embrace, and a time to refrain from
    embracing;
  a time to seek, and a time to lose;
  a time to keep, and a time to throw away;
  a time to tear, and a time to sew;
  a time to keep silence, and a time to speak;
  a time to love, and a time to hate;
  a time for war and a time for peace.
      For everything there is a season,
      And a time and purpose for every matter
        under heaven.

With an image of the writer of those words in Ecclesiastes for company, I spent an unforgettable New Year's Day, sitting on my grave, considering the meaning of life. I've often sat in that same place since then, as I have worked out ways to share my thinking with you. I had that photograph made on my birthday to hang on my office wall to keep me focused in my task. More than a grave, the site has become a workshop and laboratory. I go there when the muddy springs of my mind need clearing. A ritual of reckoning.

ONCE

*The most difficult mountain to cross
is the threshold.*

DANISH PROVERB

You've cleared away the dinner dishes, and you're sitting at the table with close friends having coffee and tea. A conversation about kissing in movies leads to can-you-top-this stories, beginning with the line, "I'll never forget the first time I . . ." The first-kiss and first-date tales are painfully funny. Slowly but surely, the conversation turns to deeper reflections about first times. This is more than the sharing of random memories. These stories are the accounts of crossing thresholds between stages of life. These are no less crucial than the tales pilgrims tell about crossing high mountain passes from one valley to another, on the way to some longed-for destination. Only at some distance in time and place do you understand the significance of the crossing over—finding in the ritual retelling a way of sanctifying the memory.

"I'll never forget the first time I had my period." Elizabeth, a woman in her early forties, speaks, and the shine of tears appears in her eyes. "My mother had prepared me for it. And since I was thirteen, I also knew about it from my friends who were already well into puberty. In fact, knowing exactly what it meant made the event even more powerful than if I had not known.

"When I saw the blood on my underpants, I remember thinking, So now I'm not a little girl anymore—I'm a woman. I went into the bathroom and stared at myself naked in the mirror. I couldn't have looked much like a woman, but that's what I saw. When I told my mother, she was very quiet. She must have felt the same way I did—excited and sad at the same time. She held me in her arms, and we both cried and cried. And then we laughed. And then we went shopping. My mother said, 'A *woman* has got to have CLOTHES.'

"I had owned and worn a kind of token bra since the summer when my friends all got bras, though in fact I could have gotten by with a couple of pieces of tape at most. But what I had was a kids' pretend bra—a play bra. Now I got my first serious bra— with a little reinforced shape and a little room for anticipated growth. I finally stuck out. I kept that bra long after I outgrew it. I guess it was a kind of public announcement of my new status. I wouldn't be surprised if my mother has it somewhere—she probably had it bronzed.

"I'm sure my mother told my father what had happened, because at dinner that night he was very serious and formally polite. I suppose he knew what I knew. But nothing was said between us. I do remember that I was treated at the table like the young woman I felt I had become. Childhood was over.''

ᏜᏜ

"I'll never forget the first time I deliberately turned to crime." Ernie, a man in his mid-thirties. "I think of it as my Adam experience—when despite everything I'd been told and everything I knew, I deliberately did what I was told to never, ever do. And I did it all at once. I stole money from my mother's purse, crossed three streets I was forbidden to cross, went shopping for forbidden candy at the neighborhood grocery, and stole the candy instead of paying for it. I must have been six and a half—in my first year in school. I remember how scared and excited I was—the defiance of rules had such power in it. Even more powerful was the fact that I didn't get caught. Not the first time. Not even the *second* time.

"But the third time, my mother caught me. She'd found candy wrappers in my pants pockets and extra change in my schoolbag the previous night, so she was lying in wait for me when I snuck into the house after school. Where had I been and what had I been doing? I lied. She searched me. Busted. She whipped me, lectured me, marched me up to the grocery store to confess, made me ask forgiveness from the grocer there and then and also forgiveness from God over evening prayers. In a strange way, she was merciful.

She said she wouldn't tell my father this time, but if I did it again, she would tell him for sure, and he would kill me.

"Getting caught and punished didn't seem all that big a deal, really. I knew that happened. I saw it every day in school. It did impress me that while it was OK for God to know what I did, my mother would deceive my father about it.

"Still, the watershed moment was that first experience of theft and lie—having learned that sometimes you can deliberately do something wrong and not get caught. Right and wrong became a matter of weighing the chances and consequences of getting caught. Knowing that I could play with fire and not always get burned was the path that has led to trouble ever since."

∽

"I didn't want to bring this up when you asked the question the other night. This example seems so damned dumb, but it's really important to me." Steve, a balding man in his middle years. "I never will forget the morning when I changed the part of my hair from one side of my head to another.

"I was born with what my mother called a cowlick—an unruly shock of hair my mother tried to plaster down on one side of my head. She was so concerned about this that I felt a cowlick was some kind of unattractive and unfortunate birthmark. She parted the hair on the right side of my head.

"At age sixteen, I spent a summer away from home working for a tree farmer. Terribly conscious of how young I looked, I tried growing a beard—no luck. And I tried combing my hair in some other fashion—swept back, parted in the middle, slicked up in the back. The moment I moved the part to the other side of my head, I felt as if I had also moved my mother out of a part of my life. And besides, it worked wonders for my looks—the cowlick worked *for* me instead of against me.

"It was such an important act for me. From that moment on, I combed my hair the way it pleased me, cowlick or no cowlick. My way.

"For forty years I combed my hair that way, and every time I did, I pushed my mother away from me. There was much she didn't like about my life—and the parting of my hair became a ritual parting of the ways with her.

"After our dinner-table conversation last week, I did something that surprised me. I parted my hair back on the side of my childhood. It actually looks better and combs more naturally; the cowlick problem is now of no consequence because I'm bald in the front and the problem hair is gone.

"Not only that, but my need to defy my mother is gone as well.

"The only issue now is how does it look—not who decides.

"So, for a week now, I've been parting my hair as it was as a child. Nobody has noticed—not even my wife or closest friends. Why should they? It means nothing to them. But it's a big deal for me. I'm finally relieved of some nagging, irritating burden. This new ritual of combing my hair as naturally as possible makes me smile, and leaves me strangely at ease. I look forward to combing my hair each morning as I please. It's a sign I am finally an independent adult.''

∽

As for me, I'll never forget the first time I voted in a real election—a presidential election: 1960. Because I was born in 1937, my political awareness was dominated by Roosevelt, Truman, Eisenhower, and the impact of the Second World War. It was my parents' time and world.

With Eisenhower fading into old age and history, and the fifties coming to an end, I celebrated my twenty-first birthday just before the contest for the presidential election of 1960 began to dominate national politics. It was my generation's turn, and my generation was ready. From early on, I supported John Fitzgerald Kennedy, working in his campaign in a small and local way. I admit that part of my enthusiasm came from his being unacceptable to my parents; he was so young—younger than they were by far—and he was *Catholic*.

When he was nominated by the Democrats, I was overjoyed. I watched the Nixon/Kennedy debates with intense interest and concern. The pundits of the press said this was going to be close—every vote counted. That meant me—I counted.

I was first in line at the voting booth that November morning. So wound up, I was shaking. I had never been in a voting booth before. But this was more than voting—this was an event in the making of history—an act to validate all my hopes for the future. I was carried away with self-importance as I solemnly stepped into the little booth with all the dignity of a student about to receive a diploma. Pulling the gray curtain behind me, I stared at the machine in fear. What if I make a mistake? I took forever to read the instructions and get each vote right. Saving the presidential vote for last, I voted—and pulled the validating lever with a mighty sound of "CHUNG." Yes! I had done it. I threw back the curtain and walked out into the morning sunshine, feeling as though I and I alone had cast the deciding vote for Kennedy. An anxious youth had walked into that voting booth, and Citizen Fulghum had walked out, having taken his decisive place in the affairs of the people.

When my children were young, I always took them with me when I voted.

A family ritual of responsibility.

Even now I carry my voter-registration card in my wallet—reminding me of both my privileges and my obligations as an adult citizen in a free country. The card tells me much more than just the location of my voting booth. It's one of the most powerful talismans of my identity—even more important than a driver's license.

Anybody can drive a car.

∾

"I'll never forget the first time I had sex." Charlotte, a gentle, dignified woman in her early fifties. "Looking back, it seems like such a brief moment— like jumping off a cliff and not getting hurt. I know I did what I wasn't supposed to do. And I know I was lucky—nothing awful happened. Still, it's a keep-sake memory.

"In reality, having sex the first time almost consumed the last three months of my senior year in high school. My older sisters told me all about sex, and I found out about masturbation and orgasm on my own. But I was more than just interested. There was this mad urge—this upwelling of lust so insistently strong that I decided if the right boy came along, I was going to let him do more than kiss me.

"Mr. Right turned out to be a guy who had just come to our school the previous fall. He'd moved to town with his parents from New York City. Stan. Stanley. Oh, my. He was so different, so cool, so sexy. He smoked Lucky Strike cigarettes and wore a leather jacket. Flattop haircut, ducktails in the back. Oh, Stanley, where are you now?

"Anyhow. When we saw each other in our bathing suits at a swimming party that spring, we must have had the same thought at the same time, because about a week later we were out on a date and at the same lake in the middle of the night making out like animals in the front seat of a 1936 Ford—kissing and touching and licking and sucking—kept from going all the way only by the presence of the other couple in the backseat, who were doing the same thing and not doing the same thing for the same reasons we were.

"Stan invited me to the senior prom, and I knew why and what for. Yes.

"I really don't remember the dress I wore or anything else about the prom itself. I do remember leaving the dance early, going out to the lake, stripping down to our underwear to swim, taking off our underwear in the water and touching and feeling everywhere, and having sex right there in the water. A wave of feeling hit me. I felt so weak I thought I'd drown.

"I can see that moment so clearly still—two kids there in the water—holding on tight to each other—overwhelmed, satisfied, scared, and exhausted. He laughed, and I cried—for the same reasons, I suppose. It was the first time for both of us. We had both lost our virginity, forever.

"It was the most powerful event of my senior year. Not even the actual graduation ceremony could compare. Sitting there in my little cap and gown, I felt silly. High school was over. I was a woman now."

☙

Nobody says, "*We* never will forget the first time *we* . . .*"

The most powerful dimension of the threshold experience is solitary.

"I will never forget the first time I . . ." is the marker of self, alone.

It emphasizes your separateness from others.

Lifelong, there are uncountable first times that define you.

The first time you walk home alone from school, with a little time all your own. The first time you are left alone at home as a child—not having to go with your mother on errands. The first time you are allowed to be alone at home in the evening without a baby-sitter. And even more liberating, the first time your parents are away overnight or for a weekend, and the house is all yours.

On your own. Strong moments—scary and exciting.

∞

Without much effort, I've collected enough of these first-time stories to fill a book. Stories of baptism, joining the Scouts, and initiation into a sorority. Stories of catching parents in a lie or deception, or catching parents making love. Stories of sleeping away from home for the first time, the first dance, and the first sexual encounter. Learning to tie shoelaces, learning something by heart, learning the news of the death of a friend or parent. "I'll never forget the first time I . . .'' is followed by accounts ranging from getting the first real job, to being elected to an office in school, to finding out you are pregnant with your first child.

These passages will be matched in later years when you experience your parents' side of the ritual separation. Finding out how pleasant it is to not always have a kid tagging along. Experiencing the bittersweet disengagement of your last child moving out of the house, leaving you once again home alone in your house. And in old age, realizing you can no longer drive alone or go downtown alone—that you have done those things alone for the last time.

There are no parties or gifts or certificates to mark these times.

Most often, nobody else knows or takes notice.

But you know. You, alone.

Sometimes it's wonderful. Sometimes awful. Sometimes both.

But never trivial.

Ꮼ

The moment when something of importance happens to you, for the first or only time, may not be recognized at the time as a rite of passage or a ritual event. Only much later will you see its crucial moment in the scheme of things.

There is an exact word for this phenomenon: ''liminality.''

''Liminality'' is the word for the threshold moment—from the Latin root *limin,* meaning the centerline of the doorway. Liminality is the moment of crossing over. It describes the transitional phase of personal change, wherein one is neither in an old state of being nor a new, and not quite aware of the implications of the event.

All the stages of life include liminality.

Life is nothing but moments of crossing over.

Stitching these moments together into the comforting quilt of wisdom is the task of one's later years.

Only with the passage of time, the accumulation of information about the similar experiences of others, and the opportunity to fit a given moment into the overall scheme of one's life does a threshold experience become understood. Then we know that the rite of passage is contained in a single move in a single moment.

Upon reconsideration, we invest the past with meaning.

This is ritual action—the ritual of remembering and revisiting the thresholds.

෨෨

Last night a married couple in their seventies came to dinner at our house and stayed late into the evening, sitting by a fire, drinking coffee and talking. They opened a bottle of the wine of their lives—and shared a glass with us. "When we were young . . . ," and "We used to . . . ," and "I'll never forget . . ."

This is not just storytelling. It is the sharing of personal mythology. It's how we all make sense out of our lives and give its events significance. It parallels the mythmaking of the human race. It is the ritual of remembrance.

As I listened to the couple talk—not infrequently at the same time—I realized they had sanded and shaped each story again and again—embellished upon, subtracted from, and repaired as necessary. They could have made a tape of what they told and simply given it to friends, if all they wanted to do was share anecdotes. But it was their need to revive and relive those times that elevated the stories to the status of parable, legend, and allegory.

The couple told of a near escape from death in an automobile accident; of a time when a dimension of the supernatural entered their lives, as prayer was answered; of a great triumph where defeat was turned into success, as a failing business deal was saved by sheer grit; and the moment when invincibility became finitude, when nothing they could do would keep a newborn child alive. They spoke of the turning point when the gathering together of possessions turned to a letting go of possessions, as they moved from the old home to a condominium—a time of collecting stones and a time of letting the piles of stones go.

Old, old stuff—for them and for the human race.

A time for all things.

The next morning, I experienced the budding phase of this ritual of remembrance when I talked on the phone with my five-year-old granddaughter, who was home from school for a day with a sore throat.

"Grandpa, tell me again about the horseback ride, when the horse ran away." I remember. It was the first time she had ridden a horse alone, without being led. The horse trotted off a little ways on its own, and she had pulled up on the reins to stop it. First we had lived that story, and then we had recounted that story the next day and several times since. A year later comes the request to tell it again. The actual event has acquired heroic dimensions. At this distance, I realize it's become mythical—a story about becoming independent, about bravery when scared, about adventure and the taming of a wild beast. We will tell it again. And again. And someday it will change form and begin, "Well, I never will forget the time, when I was a little girl, my grandfather and I went horseback riding and the horse ran away over the hills and . . ."

ᏕᏕ

No matter how personally unique the details may be or how idiosyncratic the telling may become, the great themes of myth and religion are revealed if you look at each person's ritual of remembrance with a wide-angle lens. These personal events contain the universal themes that tie us to humanity, past, present, and future. The ritual is in the remembering—the remembering is self-revelation.

Though we tend to share the events of our personal odyssey, it is not necessary to the ritual of remembrance. We do not need to construct public rituals for many of the most important moments of our lives—the ones initially observed in secret. Our lives are rich with these occasions. It is enough to know that our parents and our children and our friends and most other people pass through these same doors.

Rituals do not always involve words, occasions, officials, or an audience. Rituals are often silent, solitary, and self-contained. The most powerful rites of passage are reflective—when you look back on your life again and again, paying attention to the rivers you have crossed and the gates you have opened and walked on through, the thresholds you have passed over.

I see ritual when people sit together silently by an open fire.

Remembering.

As human beings have remembered for thousands and thousands of years.

REUNION

Return to old watering holes for more
than water—
friends and dreams are there
to meet you.

AFRICAN PROVERB

▲

THE CLASS OF
NINETEEN-EIGHTY FIVE
OF BROADVIEW HIGH SCHOOL
INVITES YOU TO ATTEND ITS

Tenth Reunion

EIGHT P.M. - JUNE 5, 1995
HIGH SCHOOL GYM
DINNER/DANCING
RSVP

▼

HIGH SCHOOL

"Come to the reunion!" Does that invitation open your mental scrapbook and put the movie of your adolescence on rerun? The most common public ritual of reunion is this one, the high school reunion.

As I write these words, many of my classmates of forty years ago are about to assemble on June 17 for the reunion of the Class of 1954 of Waco High School.

I've thought more about high school reunions than most of my former classmates, because I was a high school teacher myself for twenty years and have been invited many times to attend the tenth-year class reunions of former students. I have also been the chairman of many of the annual commencement events, working closely with each class as they planned their graduation. I had an insider's view of what was going on in the lives and minds of the students as they left high school. And I always looked forward with great interest to seeing them again at their tenth-year reunion. Teachers want to know what difference they made in the lives of their pupils, and reunions are a great place to find out.

When the students walked across the stage and out the door of high school, they were around eighteen years old, single, parent-dependent, living at home, and full of anxious plans and hopeful expectations.

By the time ten years roll around, the students have learned the lessons only experience can teach. Now they are twenty-eight—pushing thirty. College either worked out or it didn't. Jobs or careers have happened or not. Love, marriage, family, children, and home have likely become realities—even come and gone already. Most of those who are gay or lesbian have come out. Some graduates have even gone full circle by the end of ten years and are once again living with their parents.

Faces and bodies have matured and even show early signs of aging. For all appearance of enthusiasm they may wear to the reunion, they are a more sober lot since last I saw them. They know the powerful part played in their lives by luck, circumstance, and the coming and going of love. They know a good deal more now about pain and sorrow, success and defeat, debt and gain, and the price paid for getting what they thought they wanted.

The high school reunion event is a powerful ritual occasion, whether you decide to go or not. And the real reunion is not with other people so much as it is with yourself. Daily, we reunite with self in the bathroom mirror. The first high school reunion is an invitation to look into a larger mirror.

Students tell me that the arrival of the invitation comes as a shock. Have ten years really gone by? Can it really be time? This wake-up call to the passage of time is the first step in the reunion ritual.

The next step is to find their high school yearbook. To first look for themselves. And then to review those years laid out in photographs.

Then comes the big decision: to attend or not?

Students tell me that the self-searching that happens between opening the invitation and making a decision about going is, to use their phrase, "heavy stuff." A deep deliberation. It is not about high school. It is about *Who am I?* and *What has become of me?*

–

When I attend these ten-year high school reunions, I go early and station myself near the door. I want to see the entrance each person makes. When they went out the door, they were dressed alike in cap and gown. Even the hairstyles expressed a conformity.

When they walk through the door at the reunion, the costume announces who they are now—what they've become on their own. There are wide differences in attire now. They wear their adult disguises. A lot more careful attention has been paid to this entrance than they may admit. But the new clothes and shoes, the careful makeup, the fresh haircuts, and the companions they bring with them give them away. They come looking good. They come to say, ''Here I am, *now*—what do you think?''

Often, the most important persons they want to see are those whom they loved during high school. Most all of us have former girlfriends or boyfriends who still shine in our memories. We've even thought about calling them up from time to time. Where are they now? What are they like after all these years?

We also want to see the wives, husbands, lovers, or companions the former loves have brought to the reunion. Those mates also have a ritual interest in the reunion—they want to see their companion's past. Usually, the current companions will go to one reunion—after that, no way—it's not *their* high school past.

What of those students who do not return?

Their absence is a telling statement about who they are now. The nonattendees often seek out former classmates to see how the reunion went—they still want to look into the mirror . . . but in private.

Whatever comes of the high school reunion, it's an encounter with finitude—the brevity of life. The most common response I get to the question, ''So you went—what do you think?'' is this one: ''All of a sudden, I realized how quickly time passes, how fast my life is going by, how much I've already aged. I can't believe it.''

಄

A college reunion is like a high school reunion, only more so.

My wife has just returned from the twenty-fifth reunion of her college class.

When she came home, she talked for two days and is still working through the experience. She's going with a friend to a Grateful Dead concert tonight— something she would not have done before the reunion. Revisiting the music of one's youth is part of the reunion with self. Whatever your parents may have thought of the music, however the music may survive the test of time, if it was the music you listened to in high school or college days, then it plays forever in some ballroom of your mind. You can still mouth the words and do the dances.

My wife's moment of truth at the reunion was the memorial service for the members of her class who had died. Twenty of them. She's a doctor, and she knows about death. But this was different. Twenty people her age—people she knew, people like her— had already come to the end of their lives. Finitude. Life is short.

And like most of those who go to such occasions with their eyes open, she came home with a revived sense of what is consequential and who is significant and what she wanted to do with the rest of her life. A new set of hopes and dreams tempered now by the view from the middle of life and the experiences of the road taken so far.

She compared her life to her peers' and saw what

there was to like about herself and what she still might become. And in seeing how time and experience had molded some seemingly confused and useless college students into pretty fine and serviceable human beings, she felt good, knowing she was one of those.

And I am a beneficiary of her reunion, even though I did not go.

She saw the men she might have married.

And is glad she waited for me.

∽

Some people never go to the reunions or go just once. Some regret going. And there are those who attend every reunion occasion that comes up as long as they live. Whatever you are inclined to do, I have formed a strong opinion out of my experience:

The *odds* are in *favor* that the re-view in the mirror will lead you to the kind of self-revelation we associate with wisdom.

Which is why I always say you should go at least once. Go and see who you *were* or else you will never fully understand who you *are* and who you yet *may become.* The mirror always has something to tell you.

FAMILY

Let's draw a distinction between a family reunion and reunion with family. They are not the same experience. One is a gathering of relatives. The other is a reconciliation with members of our family.

We all begin with the family that fate has assigned us and then leave that family in various ways, at least for a time, and go out on our own. We often look for what's missing in our blood relationships and marry into or adopt a new family. At some stage, there comes the need for reunion or reconciliation with those we left behind. We call it "going home again."

The classic form of this ritual is contained in an old, old story, kept alive in our cultural tradition because it is constructed out of our deepest longings. I'll give you a modern version.

༄

There was this young guy—call him Jack—who decided to leave home. His parents had mixed feelings about it. Of course, they wanted him to grow up and be his own man, but they also thought it was too soon—he was still so young, maybe he should finish college first or at least just get his own apartment on the other side of town.

The young man thought his parents were too domineering and couldn't see how grown up he really was. Not only did he want to leave home, he wanted to get as far away from home as possible. And never come back. Furthermore, he wanted to take his share of the family resources with him to stake his future.

There was a full-force family fight over dinner one night. Hard words, the throwing down of napkins, chairs pushed away, and a walking away in different directions, slamming doors behind. It left family unity as dead and picked-over as the roast chicken on the platter.

Nothing the father could say would change the son's mind. Finally, in the kitchen before he left for work the next morning, he asked his wife to give the kid some money—he washed his hands of the whole mess. He'd done all a father knew how to do. To hell with him. The father privately thought he should have raised dogs instead of kids—at least the dogs would be dead by now. The father was bitter.

Now the mother knew two things that neither the father nor the son would admit: one, the son was just like his old man, and two, his old man had run away from home when he was about the same age and joined the navy. She also knew it was not the time to bring these matters to the attention of the son or the father.

She wrote a check. Tearfully, she gave it to her son. Watched him throw his baggage into the back of his old car and drive off. It broke her heart to see him go.

The son didn't write. Or call.

The mother grieved and worried. The father

cursed the day he had ever had a second son. His older son was not like this rebel. The older son stayed home, finished his education, married a nice girl, had a nice son of his own. This son came to work in the family business, came over to eat Sunday lunch and watch football on the TV. He helped his father chop wood in the fall and prune the fruit trees in the early spring. He never forgot birthdays, Mother's Day, or Father's Day. He even painted the garage, on his own, to surprise his father, for no good reason at all. The Good Son. God bless him.

Meanwhile. The younger son went to San Francisco, got a job in a restaurant waiting tables, rented a small apartment, and spent his spare time hanging around the music scene. He slept with quite a few women. He started drinking and doing drugs, lost his job, sold his car and possessions, and ended up on welfare. In desperation he found work washing dishes in a nightclub, and slept on the floor on a mattress in a back room. His health deteriorated, but he had no money for a doctor. Hungry, hungover, sick, lonely, depressed, and friendless, he began to think of home.

One day he borrowed money from the nightclub manager and rode twenty hours on a bus, arriving in his hometown on a Sunday morning. Alone and unrecognized, he walked around town—down the main street, past his grade school and high school, past the church where he had been an acolyte, and finally, he turned onto the street where he grew up. Slowly, he walked toward home. He was scared, so scared. "What if they don't want me? . . ."

Many a time his father had sat alone in the front-porch swing, looking down the street. His father had composed severe speeches in his mind: If that damned kid ever showed up, he'd strip a few pieces of hide off him—how dare he leave and never write or call! These hot speeches masked his grief and anguish. God forbid something awful should have happened to his son.

His father saw him coming.

As if in a dream, he stood up, walked slowly down the sidewalk.

The son saw his father coming to meet him.

As the father lifted his arms and held them outspread, the son did the same and ran and threw his arms around his father. His father pulled back from the embrace long enough to look in his son's face. It was the first time the son had ever seen his father cry. "Welcome home," he said. "Welcome home."

ᏇᎲ

The parable of the Prodigal Son has many interpretations.

The story lives on because it contains elemental human truths about the stages of reunion: separation, alienation, forgiveness, acceptance, and blessing. Our own family reunion experiences may vary in intensity and vary in details, but not in basic form.

This old story goes to the heart of reunions with

family. The rite of passage is that moment of crossing over from separation to reconciliation between
members of a family—most powerfully between
child and parent. And even if it never happens—even
if the reunion isn't completed—it's universal that we
want it to happen.

"I'm sorry."

"I forgive you."

"It's all right—we'll work it out."

"I love you—no matter what."

This is the language of the ritual of reconciliation.

It is what we want, what we need . . . what we
long for.

⊗

Sometimes the ritual of separation and reunion is
subtle.

A friend has a powerful mother. She has stood in
awe of her mother all her life and has no rational
cause to feel anything but respect for her. She is a
good mother. The daughter is a good daughter. Her
mother reciprocates the respect. They are proud of
one another. On the surface, you would see the evidence. The observance of family rituals is formally
reliable. Birthdays, anniversaries, and seasonal holidays have always been observed with cards and gifts.
And they have always maintained a regular corre-
spondence by letter and phone.

Yet the mother and daughter have not been close
since early childhood—never really intimate. And

the daughter has spent most of her life living away from her mother. The daughter has never felt there was anything her mother needed from her. And the mother has felt she raised her daughter well, and her daughter could make her own way in the world without any help and handle the consequences of her decisions on her own. Or so they've said.

They have a workable relationship. But not a satisfactory one.

Last year the mother had a stroke and was hospitalized for several weeks. For the first time, she confronted her own finitude—realized that she will die. The father was thrown for a loss—demobilized by his wife's illness. Now, for the first time, the daughter stepped into their lives as the strong and capable member of the family, taking charge of family affairs and dealing with the emotional needs of her father and mother. The intimacy long missing between them came to life.

Sitting for hours at her mother's bedside, the daughter observed the ritual of remembrance—sorting through her life with her parents, seeing her mother as another human being, considering her mother's life in light of her own experiences.

She and her mother saw one another in each other's mirrors. In some unspoken way, her mother let go of thinking she always had to be the family rock and passed the responsibility on to her daughter. The daughter accepted. She, too, was ready to cross the threshold.

This ritual of the passage of power is never planned, really. When it happens with grace, there is reunion of a very special kind. The strings that bind the mother and daughter have been retied with the timely bow of another stage of life. They have welcomed one another home.

෮෨

It doesn't always work out this way. I know.

Both my parents died without any reconciliation between us. I, their only child, did not live up to their expectations. Nor did they to mine. I wish it had not been so, and they must have felt the same way. The ritual of reunion never happened. The distance between us was so great that I didn't even attend their funerals.

Though I have tried to sort through that story to make sense of it, I cannot. Perhaps when I am older and wiser, I will understand. I only mention this because it is important to acknowledge how much I empathize with those for whom reunion remains an unfulfilled hope. Some things, when broken, cannot be fixed.

My parents probably wanted to welcome me home as deeply as I wanted to be welcomed. Now, in my later years, I sympathize with their sadness when, from time to time, a distance develops between me and one of my children.

I also know now that the ritual of reconciliation is forever intertwined with the ritual of rebellion. And I know that both rituals are likely to repeat themselves several times over in my children's lives and mine.

Make no mistake: While these are not ritual events to which engraved invitations are sent, they are nevertheless rites of passage of great significance. The coin with which they are paid is pain—sometimes bitter, sometimes sweet, but pain, nonetheless. Nobody gets a free and easy ride.

৩৯

At times, family reunion of the most solemn and serious nature is the underlying ritual for gatherings that are given other names and held for other reasons: Thanksgiving, High Holy Days, Christmas, birthdays, weddings, graduations, backyard barbecues, and funerals.

And then, there's the Big One—the family reunion that happens around the fiftieth wedding anniversary of a couple who by now are great-grandparents—when *everybody* comes.

There must be some deep magnetism well below consciousness that draws related people together in these circumstances—something to do with genetic suction. The twisted helical complexity of the structure of DNA is more than an accidental model for what goes on around a family gathering.

It is compounded by what happens when you marry—you add all these other people to your life because you love their relative. It's heartening when your in-laws seem to be a better deal as a family than your own. Of course. There's no baggage from the past to carry. Ah, true, but the baggage is on the way.

I love the wedding and fiftieth wedding anniversary photographs with every member of both families all gathered together. You can see the truth in their faces. In more than one way, they are assuming a pose. Many of these people do not know each other. Some of the people who do know each other dislike each other. Many of these people do not want to be there and are not sure just why they are there. And many of them know that the others know that they know these truths. But, there they are. Smiling, smiling.

The reason they are there: "We just have to go."

And they "just have to go" to funerals and Thanksgiving and all the rest. It's asking for trouble to say, "I think your relatives are boring, and you can tell them I said so," or "I am never going to be in the same room with your mother again," or "They'll never change." You still have to go.

What amazes me is that we so often pull it off. We do.

The yearning is so strong within us for family integrity that we will go to great lengths to make the unlikely work out. We will compromise, conciliate, and accommodate over and over and over. We will go because we just have to go—because we need to believe that this time it will be OK. And sometimes, over time, it is. These family gatherings are not a celebration of the way things really are, but a ritual of hope—aimed at what we devoutly wish things to be.

This hope—this lifelong reaching—is why we do things that cause other people to say, ''I can't believe you did that.'' It sends us off on long vacations with our parents and our children in the same car, even when we know what we're getting into. It rallies us to get everybody together for our parents' wedding anniversaries or big-deal birthdays. It carries us across country to some distant relative's funeral, knowing everybody else in the family will have to be there, too. It makes us start sending birthday cards to relatives we hold in so-so esteem.

And for all the times I have sensed and heard, ''God, I hope we don't ever have to go through that again,'' I have seen family war spears plowed under the ground of the goodwill that the passage of time and the human capacity for growth sometimes achieve. The ritual event sometimes results in that which is hoped for: a sense of re-connection—of belonging. We go to the family reunion and are, much to our surprise and satisfaction, finally, at peace with these people—home again.

ADOPTION

I'm really uneasy about telling this next story. It concerns an adoption in my own family. Part of me says to keep it to myself, and another part says there is good reason to share. I will feel better if I explain both why I'm telling such a personal story and why I will leave out some of the details.

For one thing, I've learned how many adoptions there are and how many lives are affected by a single adoption. There are nearly 7 million legally registered adoptions, as well as many that are not recorded. Directly involved, in addition to the child, are the two biological parents of the child and the two adoptive parents, as well as any siblings. If the adopted child eventually marries and has children, the spouse and children are also directly affected by the adoption experience of the parent. And where do you draw the line? If you add in the children who go with one parent in a divorce situation and are adopted by the new spouse, you've got a large percentage of the population not raised by both their biological parents. Adoption, like divorce, is a substantial part of our social structure—a fact of life in American culture.

Yet adoption is often a carefully kept family secret.

And I know how awful it can be to live with family secrets.

It may be useful for me to tell my own story and share my experience. This story also belongs to all those directly involved, and I am careful not to invade their privacy. I've a right only to my story, not theirs. But they have read the story you are about to read and are comfortable with what I've written and why.

∽

I've never known anybody who didn't have a skeleton or two in their closet. You know it's there—and you get in the closet with it from time to time—a reunion with pain, sorrow, or demons. There are always those things we don't want to talk to anybody about. Shame, guilt, and embarrassment are the locks on the closet door.

Over time, if all goes well, we come to terms with the skeletons in a way that allows our lives to go on. When things don't go well, we turn to others for help with the rattling bones. Despite our own desire to keep our secrets secret, we are all comforted and relieved when we find out most everybody else is in the same fix as we are—almost everybody has a closet, a locked cabinet, or drawer somewhere.

Here's something I'm sure of: Whether the skeleton is in or out of the closet, there is still anguish and suffering. Even if injuries heal, the scar tissue is always tender, and the wound may be reopened easily.

When it comes to family secrets, the problem is compounded because you are a co-owner of the skeleton. Other people are involved. It's not just your story to tell—your skeleton to expose and bury—it's theirs, too.

Leaving the matter in the closet is painful, but so is taking it out. You may heal yourself at the expense of damaging others in your family.

If you are adopted and seek your birth parents,

your showing up may prove unwelcome and destructive. It happens.

If you're gay and come out of the closet to seek your own wholeness, your family may be divided and even destroyed. It happens.

If you've committed a crime and seek to rectify it, you may cause more trouble than you ever imagined possible. It happens.

On the other hand, great good may come of great pain if it heals in the healthy atmosphere truth can provide. This happens, too.

And when good comes of exorcising the demons, other people, seeing, may take heart and clean out a closet of their own.

In this spirit, I tell you my story.

࿐

Thirty-seven years ago, when I was twenty, I was engaged to marry. Announced at Christmas, the wedding was set for the following August.

In the spring of that year, my fiancée and I succumbed to the power of love and passion, so that by the time of the wedding she was four months pregnant, though, for some complicated reasons, we didn't realize it at the time.

Today, a pregnant bride is not so unusual. For better or worse, society seems to be far more comfortable with a wide variety of timing when it comes to the bearing of children. But not in 1958. Not in small-town Texas.

My fiancée and I had been raised in an environment of strict fundamentalist religion and narrow social values. We were ignorant in sexual matters, on less than intimate terms with our parents, and about to make a major break with our cultural roots by going off to graduate school in California.

When we discovered she was pregnant, we panicked. It's hard to reconstruct our state of mind from this distance, but I know we were scared, unready for childrearing, fearful of parental rejection despite our defiant need for independence, ashamed, confused, and dazed.

We hid the fact of pregnancy from everyone— friends as well as family—easy to do if you've just moved to a new city far from home. As if nobody else had ever faced this dilemma, we sought no counsel, concluding there was no choice but to place the baby for adoption. We contacted a social-service agency and made the necessary arrangements. Three days after the child was born, we went home without her. The agency placed her with a family who wanted a child.

The birth of our daughter and the relinquishment of her were soul-searing experiences. It was a death. Her mother and I buried all our feelings—never sorting them out between us, even to this day.

Life went on—we grew up, two sons were born to us. And we adopted a daughter—because we wanted to be certain of having a girl, and perhaps because we wanted to balance some equation in our hearts between sadness and joy.

Despite this reaching for family, our marriage failed, and we divorced. She remarried, happily, and so did I.

Over the years, we each accommodated ourselves, at least on the surface, to the sorrows around the birth and relinquishment of that first child.

But the memory of that child did not fade. I found myself celebrating the child's birthday each year. A secret anniversary—January 16—observed with a ritual walk, alone, to imagine what the child was like, what the child must be doing, where the child must be living.

I knew when she must be going to school, passing through puberty, entering high school, graduating, going out into the world, falling in love—the whole story. The child existed in my imagination as surely as if I had all the facts of her life.

Not knowing what had become of her haunted me, pained me, grieved me.

I wanted to find her. But I felt I had no right, and that my appearance would be unwelcome, if not damaging. I could not look for her, though I often was tempted. Both searching and not-searching vexed me.

What if she was in trouble, had a terrible life, needed me now? What if she was looking for me? What if she never wanted to know about me? What should I do? A tenacious dilemma—and my life's great sorrow.

Sometime after I assumed she was an adult, I began to unburden myself—telling friends, a counselor, and, finally, my other children. It seemed to me there would never be a reunion. Some things one has to live with; there is no choice—some things cannot ever be undone. I felt the same way when my parents died—I knew a homecoming was permanently out of the question.

The January I knew she turned thirty, I decided the story would remain unresolved, and I was conscious of ritually laying my grief to rest in a far corner of my heart.

—

During the year when *All I Really Need to Know I Learned in Kindergarten* achieved recognition, the adoptive parents of my child read the book. They knew my name and enough about me to know that the author and I must be the same person. After careful thought, they decided to tell their daughter what they knew.

I know now that this decision was a reflection of their love for her—a love that made it possible for them to let her know and let her go to find the missing pieces of her identity. They would not lose a child in the process, but the child would find a missing part of herself—no more and no less than what any parent wants. They trusted that their child would come back to them knowing who her parents are and have always been and why: those who wanted her, adopted her, cared for her, reared her, and who love her still. And so it has been.

—

And so the telephone call came:
"Are you Robert Fulghum?"
"Yes."
"Did you place a child for adoption in 1958?"
"Yes."
"I think I'm your daughter."
"Yes!"
Stunned, I wept and walked around in a daze. I could hardly believe it.

She came to Seattle the following Wednesday.

Because I was arriving from an out-of-town trip later the same evening, she was met at the airport by other members of my family. A little later I came straight from the airport to my first wife's house and parked a block away, thinking I would walk a little and compose my mind.

Instead, I ran—as hard as I could run—rushed through the front door and into the living room—the prodigal father, come to the reunion.

—

It's enough to tell you that she has had a fine life, has wonderful parents, and has important accomplishments to her credit. Married now, teaching at a university.

The rest of the story will be unfolding for a long time to come.

Relationships always take time. Always.

If I've dealt with all this reunion in an intelligent way, no small part of the credit goes to the staff of a remarkable institution, the Hope Cottage Adoption Center in Dallas, Texas. By coincidence I made a connection with them just after my daughter and I were reunited. Invited to speak for the agency at a fund-raising event, I spent time in its offices, where I shared my story with its staff and asked for advice and help. This time I wanted to do the right thing.

More than being an agency devoted to placing children in families, Hope Cottage has done extensive research into the long-term effects of adoption on all those involved. The people at Hope Cottage are experienced, and compassionate. And I am in their debt for their generous, thoughtful counsel.

Their director and staff helped me understand there would be many stages of this reunion—and that, like all relationships, it would take time to establish common ground between my daughter and me.

In sum, they counseled, ''Be patient. Be kind. Be wise.''

–

Several years have passed, and much water has flowed under many bridges, and as some bridges collapse between my daughter and me, new bridges keep getting built. Her adoptive parents have been gracious in telling me their part of the story and in sharing their photographs and memories. Whatever happens in the future, the fierce anxiety of not knowing what happened to my daughter is resolved.

I have a talisman of all this—a keepsake, a piece of existential evidence of this reunion—which I value beyond any price. It's on an ordinary piece of white typing paper in a small frame on my wall. On the paper is the overlapping outline of two hands.

At the end of her first visit, when we were parting and were at a loss for words and unwilling to say good-bye, she took a piece of paper off my desk, placed my hand on it, and drew around my hand and fingers with a pen. Silently, she gave me the pen, and I placed her hand on top of the outline of my hand and drew around hers. We put our initials side by side, dated the drawing, hugged each other, smiled, laughed, cried, and she was gone—back to her parents, her home, her life.

That wordless act of the drawing of the overlapping hands was a ritual of reunion. At that threshold moment, our lives crossed again.

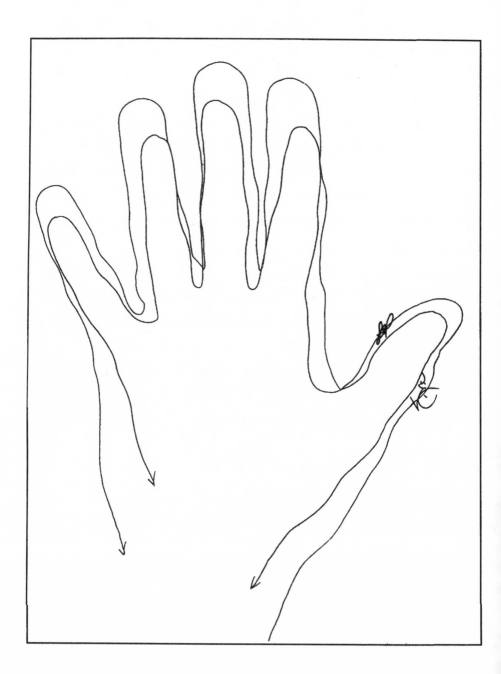

∽

COMMUNION

Once upon a time, somewhere far back in ancient human history—so far back that personal survival was the only concern—a defining event must have taken place. Someone didn't eat what he found when he found it, but decided to take it back to the cave to share with others. There must have been a first time. A first act of community—call it communion—in the most elemental form.

–

As with other important things, I learned about this in kindergarten. Or, I should say, I finally understood it by being with little children.

When my first son was in kindergarten, I was a parent volunteer who visited the school once a week to teach folk songs to the children. Singing came between naptime and snacktime. Regularly, I was invited to stay after singing and join the class for milk and cookies. I gladly stayed. Not because I was particularly hungry, but because I enjoyed watching the children carry out this ordinary task with such extraordinary care.

Since learning community cooperation is an essential part of kindergarten, the children took turns bringing cookies from home. Each day every child had an essential job in the sharing.

Two children set the table with napkins and cups. Two others arranged chairs. Others went to the refrigerator for cartons of milk, while two more fetched the cookies from the cupboard and arranged them neatly on plates. One child was responsible for placing something in the middle of the table to talk about during the snack—anything the child wished, but something the others might appreciate, as well. Show and tell.

For half the class, their job for the day was being good guests. Saying, ''Yes, please, I would like to have some milk,'' and ''Thank you very much,'' and ''How nice the table looks.'' An important task.

When all were served, everyone was expected to sit quietly for a moment, with hands folded in lap, until the teacher said, ''Let's share.'' Each ''host'' took a cookie off his plate, broke it in half, and gave it to a ''guest'' before eating the other half himself.

During this snacktime, they discussed the ''think about'' object in the center of the table—a book, a goldfish in a bowl, a toy, whatever. After the cookies and milk were consumed, the children who had played ''guests'' for the day cleaned up and put away everything, before all went out to play.

The children did this efficiently and unselfcon-sciously—it was their routine. I, too, took the event seriously. It was a high point in my week.

A lovely, sane moment with people—never mind our difference in age.

The finest, simplest elements of civilization at work.

It served as an example of the way daily habits become sacred rites. For me, it was communion.

The sacraments are defined by the church as "out-ward and visible signs of an inward and spiritual grace." Cookies and milk with those children be-came a sacrament for me. Grace was clearly present. It was a ritual reminder that civilization depends on sharing resources in a just and humane fashion. This is not kid stuff.

—

To speak of sharing milk and cookies with chil-dren as a communion experience may verge on blas-phemy in the eyes of some. "Communion" is neither a neutral nor a simple notion for most adults who have any experience with organized religion. In our culture, it's almost impossible to separate it from two thousand years of investiture in the heart of Christianity. For Christians, communion is a sacra-ment, even though theologians debate its meaning and churches disagree on how it should be celebrated and who may join in the celebration.

I say that for *all human beings,* communion is a sacrament.

I think of communion as an act of community in spiritual fellowship, which predates all organized religion. Within the Judeo-Christian tradition, the Seder—the Passover service—was observed long before Christian communion. And before the Seder, before Jews were Jews, *people* did something like this for the same reason. It's not an act that belongs to any one group—it's ours.

Since the beginning of time, people who trust one another, care for one another, and are deeply connected to one another have shared food as a sign of and a reaffirmation of their relationship.

When attention is paid to this sharing, it takes on a ritual character.

The nurturing of the body becomes a metaphor of the mutual nourishing of lives. Every time we hold hands and say a blessing before a meal, every time we lift a glass and say fine words to one another, every time we eat in peace and grace together, we have celebrated the covenants that bind us together.

I cannot say this strongly enough: Whatever else communion may come to be, it is *an act that arises out of our humanity, not organized religion.*

–

When we speak of ''breaking bread'' with one another, we are not talking about merely parceling out the loaf. The phrase implies a conscious lack of haste in sharing a meal. Slow food, not fast food. Attention will be paid—to the food, to the company, and to life. We will be mindful of one another. Amen.

It has become the custom in my home, especially when we have company, to catch hands around the table just before food is served, and after a moment of silence to say:

"In this house we believe the finest blessing is fine companionship during a meal. With such company as we have now, we are blessed, indeed. May God bless us all. Amen."

—

When Jesus, the Jewish carpenter's son from Nazareth, met for the last time with his friends and followers, they had supper together and did what Jews have always done—blessed the meal. And it was at least a deeply human experience, regardless of any theological interpretation one might place on the occasion and the gestures made there.

There was unleavened bread and wine.

One, the bread, made and eaten daily—the other, the wine, a product of time.

He must have said, in effect, "I will not be around much longer. When I'm gone and you come together, don't forget me. Keep me in your hearts and minds when you break bread and drink wine—and thereby renew the covenant we have made with one another."

This Last Supper has been and will continue to be viewed in many lights. I've no quarrel with any of these views. All are free to interpret it. However organized or even disorganized religion has chosen to understand and reenact that meal, the fact remains—it is open to the meaning one brings to it.

I only say that it, like all meaningful religious acts, rests on something essential to all human relationships. And that any group of human beings who share any food together under any circumstances are free to invest that sharing with the spirit of communion. And often do.

∾

We wrestled with this matter in the church I served for many years.

Unitarians, among others, are uncomfortable with the doctrine of transubstantiation—of bread becoming flesh and wine becoming blood. Many feel it takes away from rather than adds to the meaning of that Last Supper. Yet, my congregation was open to experiencing some similar act of community in a religious setting.

We already had some sacred habits in place to build on. At potluck dinners, we held hands, encircling the tables bearing the food we were about to eat; then we stood in silence, which was broken by singing a fivefold amen together.

Inspired by the appropriateness of this and comforted by the feelings it engendered in me and others, I thought we might look further in this direction and see where our longing led us. And though the attempts did not, in the end, succeed, the search for communion was successful as an end in itself.

∾

I invite you to consider a family church service—held at the beginning of the morning before the children go off to church school. It's the first Sunday in a new year. After the Call to Worship and some singing, the minister speaks:

The members and friends of this congregation—
    you and I—we—are tangled up with one
    another—
woven together in a unique fabric called the
    Fairview Church.
Sometimes we understand why we are here
    together.
Sometimes we don't.
Sometimes we will talk about our being in this
    place together.
Sometimes we can't.
But we keep showing up here on a pretty regular
    basis.
Because there is more of something here than
    anyplace else for us.
And that something is essential to our well-being.
That something is community—religious
    community.
Common concerns, common needs, common
    principles—these bind us together as an
    extended family.
And the tie which binds must be celebrated from
    time to time.

This is an ancient tradition—communion is its name.
An occasion when those who trust and care for one another share food together.
Communion is an act of spiritual community.
This morning we will share a tangerine—a fruit of midwinter.
Small yet bright—like our best hopes and dreams.
Both bitter and sweet—like life itself.
Nourishing—as we wish our relationships to be.
Plucked from a tree, it is a dead thing—like yesterday.
Examined, it contains seeds—like today.
Planted, the seeds contain great possibilities— like tomorrow.

The ushers will now pass among you with baskets of tangerines.
There are only enough for about a third of us to have a fruit.
Those who take a tangerine must peel it.
Someone else will take the fruit and share it so that all have a piece.
And a third of us will be responsible for the peels and seeds.
Sharing the tasks is an act of community as well.
When everyone has a few pieces of tangerine, we will say the blessing and feed one another.

Blessing (unison, seated):

We share this as an act of community;
As a sign of the covenant we have made with one
  another:
To sustain, support, encourage, and love one
  another.
May this place ever be the workshop of our finest
  endeavors,
And the cradle of our highest hopes and noblest
  dreams.
So let it be, Amen.

The congregation shares the pieces of tangerine—some with skill, some with an awkwardness that produces smiles and laughter. The sweet smell of juice floats across the room. There is some minor commotion as loose seeds roll under a chair pursued by a zealous child. Ushers pass baskets to collect napkins and peels. At the minister's gesture to rise, there is this parting affirmation:

We need each other, and so we come to this place—
To work and dance and laugh and cry and think.
We call ourselves a religious community—
Not because this place is in itself holy ground,
But because what we do here and say here and are
  here.
Make it so.
So let it be, Amen.

So how did it go? I wish I could say it was overwhelmingly successful and ever since that day the congregation observes a tangerine communion. But not so. Why? Well, it's hard to say exactly. While most people went along with the experience, and nobody actually objected, even when asked, there wasn't a groundswell of enthusiasm for that particular act of community. The congregation seemed to understand what I was getting at, but this wasn't quite it. It was messy and awkward and too much of a departure from something they knew.

"But," they seemed to say, "keep trying."

The experimentation continued. Wanting to stay on a level the children could understand, we used animal crackers one Sunday. Animal crackers have a long history. They've been around since 1890, and Nabisco hasn't changed the box since 1902. Animal crackers are often shared. Good idea. But when the crackers were passed in baskets, some small children got worked up over not having their choice of animals. The wail went up from more than one child. "I want a gorilla. How come he gets a gorilla, and I don't?" Even more unhappy were those who got a maimed animal or just a part. "I don't want a leg—I want a whole zebra!" An entire basket of animal crackers was spilled when two children tried sorting through the cookie zoo at the same time.

I could see the expressions on the faces of my congregation. They were a goodwilled, good-humored, and patient lot, but the expressions said, "Nice try, Reverend—better luck next time."

—

I don't give up easily.

We tried Gummi Bears, jelly beans, and M&M's (which do, too, melt in your hands, especially in church). The all-time lulu was something called Pop Rocks—a grape candy loaded with carbon dioxide that sort of exploded in your mouth when you bit down on it, producing a lavender froth around the lips and a purple stain on tongues that lasted a couple of days. ("What happened to your mouth?" "I went to church on the wrong Sunday.")

Then, too, there was a health problem. A family physician noted that if I was looking for a way to spread cold germs among a congregation, I had devised some genius-level methodology.

—

Many years later, three dimensions of these communion events stand out in my mind.

First of all, they are classic examples of the difficulty of constructing new rituals on top of well-established tradition. Reformation is never simple, never easy, never quick. It's easily foundered on the rocks of the past. The revision of the sacred habits of a religious community always takes time and is seldom well received by all. I find this applied to similar attempts to settle on an agreeable grace at the dinner table in my own home.

Second, the congregation really did understand what I was after. They wanted the same thing I did. They appreciated my efforts to find acts of community that would authentically express our feelings about one another. The words I used were right-on—it was the specific act that had problems, not the intention.

Finally, all these wiggy attempts produced a great deal of laughter and will long be fondly remembered and recounted by members of the congregation. That's a very important statement, not to be overlooked. This laughter is holy. You'll never convince me that Jesus and his companions did not also laugh together, even at the final supper.

Now, from this long look back, I've come to understand what I missed the first time. That shared laughter—mixed with shared purpose and longing—*that* was the act of community. The enthusiasm with which we recall our memories—the ritual of remembering—proves it. We had communion, after all. We were looking for something important together, and in the search we found the spirit of the companionship.

TALISMANS

Earlier I spoke of the drawing my daughter and I made of our overlapped hands as a "talisman," using a word that belongs in a list along with amulets, charms, and fetishes.

These words are most commonly found in anthropology texts concerning the ritual practices of so-called primitive peoples. That's a very limited view. Amulets, talismans, and charms abound in the lives of everyone in every time and place. They are physical signs of relationships with people and places and experiences. They are symbols of connection and re-connection, union and reunion with what is sacred to us. We wear them around our necks, wrists, and fingers. We carry them in our wallets, purses, and pockets. We hang them on our walls, place them on our mantels, and store them in boxes and drawers.

This afternoon my wife and I took time to collect some of these objects and assemble them in a package to send to my second son as a gesture of our support when he takes a major examination next week. We wouldn't say we were assembling talismans. But an anthropologist would smile at our naïveté.

My wife and I like to think of ourselves as intelligent, rational, educated, and fully modern in our thinking. We would testify in court that we do not believe in magic or voodoo or supernatural properties of natural phenomena.

As to the son: After nine years of education, training, and practical experience, he is sitting for his professional engineering examination, as required and prepared by the state of Washington. His field is electronic engineering with a specialty in fiber-optic applications. This is cutting-edge technical stuff. What's more, he's taking the exam early, fully knowing that the pass rate is very low the first time around. It's always been his way to risk the long shot.

As to our gift: If you opened the package, you would find a small wooden box. Lifting the lid, you'd see a faded neckerchief—the red-and-blue kind used on hiking trips. Unwrapping the neckerchief, you would find a small cloth bag, within which are these items:

· a Japanese coin
· a black-and-white African trade bead
· a very small fossilized chambered-nautilus shell
· a small stick of charred wood from a tree hit by lightning
· a little leather thong with three beads on it—one of turquoise, one of amber, and one of human bone
· a tiny bronze hand, open in blessing
· several photographs

Parting with some of these items was not easy for me.

I could tell you a long story about each one—each is connected to some important event or place in my life or the life of my son. When I die, he will find such keepsakes among my possessions and wonder what they were about. Better I should give them to him now and explain. Maybe he can use now the imagination they might provoke.

To keep your parent license active, you must always give your children some part of yourself as long as they and you live. He knows about this already, because he has two children of his own, which means he knows what's in the package from me isn't just any old stuff.

—

What's going on here?

What is this collection of objects supposed to mean?

Where did it come from?

Isn't this really a little strange?

And doesn't it seem like a rather elaborate out-of-all-proportion gesture—he's just taking a test, right?

Inside the family circle, such an event is a catalyst for a larger set of feelings that haven't been expressed in a while. We recognize, from time to time, that we take each other for granted and will seize upon almost any opportunity to express larger feelings. It's why some birthdays get wonderfully out of hand and turn into a celebration of the life of the person. This is the nature of the rites of private relationships.

෨෨

Give me access to your most personal space—desk or bureau drawers, jewelry box and closets—and I wager I could lay my hands on your own amulets, talismans, and charms. Even simpler, a glance at your fingers, wrists, neck, earlobes, pockets, purse, or wallet will turn up solid evidence that you, too, believe in magic.

Sometimes these items are put in a special place in an organized fashion—usually on a dresser top at home or a desktop or shelf at work. Little framed photographs, a rock or two, something a kid made at school, a key, a bronzed baby shoe, a little jar of dried flower petals and—well, you know. Shrines, altars. These are not accidental assemblages of sentimental detritus. They are the physical evidence of the ritual of remembrance.

In the long-distant past, it was felt that evil spirits had a palpable presence, and could enter the body through its orifices if powerful talismans were not worn to guard the doorways of our being. To protect themselves, our forefathers and foremothers wore bones through their noses and ears, wore rings and bracelets to provide a barrier to evil going up their veins, and wore necklaces bearing crosses, crescents, stars, and complex magical shapes.

Look on you and around you.

All this stuff is about ritual power.

In a rational sense, my gesture toward my son carries this invested power—the power of my love for him. But there's also the power of the second law of sympathetic magic—those things and people once closely attached continue to affect each other even though they are a long distance apart. We give each other tokens of this ongoing connection, saying, "I'm thinking of you. Remember me—keep in touch."

In a nonrational realm, this little package for my son is an acknowledgment of all those feelings and concerns and beliefs for which I have no adequate language or explanation—a gesture toward the mystery and power I only sense but cannot describe or control. It's serious business, a gift of solemn import.

༄

The most modern form of these rites of preservation is the photograph.

When people are asked what they would take with them if their house were on fire and they knew everything would burn, the most overwhelming reply is "photographs." And the older you get, the more important the photograph albums become. Little images on paper. Precious memories. You will look at the photographs again and again and again. They are the visual evidence of place and time and relationships. Ritual talismans for the treasure chest of the heart.

CONVENTIONS

Recently, I was a guest at what I now think of as a "reunion of the Church of the Burning Building." A newspaper article more literally described the event as a statewide convention of the members of professional and volunteer fire departments and their families. For me, the convention had all the marks of a religious gathering, and led me to some conclusions about the significance of our urge to come together in large groups. Conventions are a special form of reunion.

ᎧᏉ

Vocational researchers say that the profession with the highest satisfaction rate among its membership is firefighting. By and large, the firefighters like who they are and what they do. Most of the rest of us hold them in high esteem, as well.

Remember your first-grade-class field trip to the fire station?

When an elementary school teacher invited me to come along once again, I went with enthusiasm and was no less impressed than I had been fifty years ago. And I've returned on my own to talk with firefighters several times since. Members of the Volunteer Fire Department of Moab, Utah, and two retired members of the San Francisco Fire Department—a captain and a lieutenant—generously opened their lives to me. When I went to the firefighters' convention, I experienced the fervor of their sense of community.

The firefighters' motto is "Service."

Their values are courage, caring, community, knowledge, and physical fitness.

Many are cross-trained to be emergency medical technicians.

They are organized like soldiers, but their war is not against people. Their enemies are fire, destruction, disaster, and human suffering. As in combat, they eat together, sleep together, train together, and brave danger together. As in combat, they must be able to rely on one another when things go wrong. And, as in combat, they must be able to handle injury and death—to themselves and others. When they speak of a "baptism of fire," they're not using metaphor.

Off duty, they play together and socialize together.

They hold contests and competitions, combining work skills and fun.

They have their awards and commendations—even bands and drill teams.

They hone their skills into unconscious habits—until their job requirements and their way of life are one.

Firefighters become part of a larger family—and take care of their own in times of injury, death, and disaster, whether to themselves or to their wives or husbands or children.

What they do for their living gives their lives meaning and purpose and structure—which is something that most of us couldn't say. The structure and activities of their world parallel the structures and activities of a formalized religion.

I don't know if the Church of the Burning Building saves souls, but it saves lives, inspires the young, and dignifies the ideals of human community.

It's no wonder our culture observes the educational ritual of the visit to the firehouse. It's no wonder that when we ask children what they want to be when they grow up, we often get the answer: "Firefighter!" Here is a near-ideal form of human community. No wonder they come together in conventions—it's a family reunion.

༄

There are many secular churches.

I've seen several hundred in action.

You may belong to one.

If you reviewed my schedule for the last several years, you would see I have attended annual gatherings of associations of teachers, lawyers, nurses—and such organizations as the National Tire Dealers and Retreaders Association, the Bowling Proprietors of America, the American Society of Military Comptrollers, the National Paint and Coatings Association, the Rotary International, the Salvation Army, Physicians for Social Responsibility, and the National Rural Electric Co-Op Association, just to mention a few of the more intriguing ones.

They ask me to come and speak to them. I go because *I* want to see *them*. I've long been curious about what brings people together and what they do when they get there and what those gatherings have in common. It's another mirror in which I may see myself and learn something.

–

Americans are joiners.

And every association has its conventions, conferences, retreats, assemblies, seminars, convocations, or meetings.

Every city in the United States has a complex of convention facilities, and these facilities are associated with some kind of entertainment district. Las Vegas and Disney World/Orlando are extreme examples, but almost every city worth its salt has a convention center of some kind, connected to the development of the Old Town or the riverfront or some theme such as the Wild West or country music— something combining play and nostalgia.

Convention centers have become a version of the medieval cathedral, which was built with some religious purpose, of course, but of equal importance, to give status to the community, to provide jobs, to attract trade fairs, tourists, and business.

Convention centers are the basilicas of secular religion.

–

What's this all about?

We associate with other people like us to affirm ourselves. We come for people reasons, not professional reasons. Loneliness is one great burden of being a solitary human being. To spend time in the company of others who have our concerns, values, interests, beliefs, or occupation is to get confirmation of who we are—to feel connected to a larger image of ourselves.

It's true that many gatherings seem concerned only with business—with products, sales, and economic gain. What's wrong with that? What we do for a living defines much of who we are, and being with other people who make and sell potato peelers or whatever is no less important to those who come together than any other event that draws people together. The judgment of the value of the convention is made by those who are involved, not outsiders who see only the surface.

—

Consider the typical annual convention of any association.

On the surface of it, we come together to accomplish work, to share ideas, to make plans to lobby society or government on our common behalf. Every gathering, regardless of size, has a formal agenda—a program. Every gathering has business to do, speakers to hear, products to consider, and officers to elect. This work is the stated justification for the gathering. Serious purpose. A way of saying to ourselves that who we are and what we do is important.

Less publicly apparent is another agenda. We go to get away from home and office—to get a break from the ruts and be off the hook of daily routine. We go to see friends and comrades or be with wives and husbands, or to get away from same. We go to play golf or be a bit of a tourist—to see New Orleans or San Francisco or wherever.

We go to get new ideas, new energy, confirmation of who we are and what we do. This is recreation. A serious word—re-creation—a re-newal of self. If a convention is truly successful, this is what happened to you.

–

The inner group of any organization gives it a huge place in their lives.

Members of boards and committees, officers, longtime delegates, come to know each other well, see each other and work together across the years, get recognition at conventions, and receive awards and commendations. Their photographs appear in programs and newsletters, and upon retirement they are celebrated.

The result of all their involvement is a sense of importance, usefulness, and appreciation. A major part of their lives derives its meaning from this dedication to the inner community of their chosen organization. Often this inner group becomes their adopted family, their brotherhood or sisterhood, their church. At every convention, there is a time set aside when some president or chair ''wants to thank all those who made this possible.'' The group that stands are the nuns, priests, acolytes, and bishops of the church. The convention is the cumulative ritual observance of the activities that give their lives meaning and purpose—high church.

There is also an exhibit hall. A zillion dollars are spent on this dimension of a convention—where new products, new technologies, new services, new systems, are displayed. There are music and flashy displays and excitement. Books, gadgets, pamphlets, gifts, souvenirs, and demonstrations are available. Salespeople reach out to you in every creative way imaginable. It's one more way of knowing that you and your group are important and that there is a progressive, active, cutting edge to your common enterprise.

If all this weren't important to us, we wouldn't spend billions of dollars on it.

෨෧

The penultimate ritual occasion of a convention is the banquet.

In the main ballroom of a hotel, in a setting that speaks of King Arthur and his court, we sit at round tables set with fine linen, excessive silver, glasses for wine, flowers, and favors. Cocktails, music, special lighting, and decorations are added.

It ain't like this at home.

Precisely. That's why you come. That's why you dress up—suit and tie, fancy dress and makeup, jewelry, perfume, the works. Tonight is something special. And you are with special people like you.

At your table are essential elemental ritual items:

fire—in the form of candles: matter becoming
   energy
water—the metaphor of life
bread—the staff of life
sugar and salt and pepper—the sweet and savory
   and bitter
wine—the product of fermentation and time
special utensils—goblets, silver—with richness
   of purpose
and friends—members of the brotherhood and
   sisterhood
and manners—you will use your most graceful
   ritual behavior.

These items are not present by accident—they are
the necessary signs and elements of a celebrational
ritual. Pizza and beer and paper plates won't do it.
Do you remember the children in kindergarten sharing cookies and milk? We've been in training for
these occasions for a long time.

When it works well, this is reunion—coming together in convention.

The rite of self-affirmation by association—being
with people like us.

The ritual of relevance—of belonging to a community of significance.

∽

You hate these things, you say? You dread going?
It's not the conventions that are the problem.

You're involved with the wrong people.
Find your group and get in with them.

GOD

I continue to be surprised where my thinking about rituals has led me. I had not considered how often we return to a place or thing or person or concept to reconcile our relationship with it. This spiraling quest for being settled within ourselves and at home in our world lasts as long as we live.

So far, we've considered reunion with self, with friends and family, and with places and things. One more reunion: with God—or with whatever you feel that word refers to or whatever word like it that you would use to point at ultimate concerns. You may believe that God is a verb or a noun, and that God is the fundamental process of the universe or a person. In any case, we still have grounds for conversation about times of alienation from and reunion with exactly that concept or process. There are times when one is in sync with whatever gods there are, and times when anything divine or holy or sacred or ultimate seems far away, and we are lost.

This problem is pinpointed in a typewritten message I found last year stuck to the inside of the door of a toilet in a men's rest room in a seminary classroom building of the Graduate Theological Union in Berkeley, California.

God, I have a problem.
I'm just a man and I'm feeling so alone.
God, I know you have no name, but I need to call
  you something.
God, I know you are not a man like me, but I need
  to think of you that way.
God, I know you are everywhere, but I need to talk
  to you somewhere.
God, I know you are eternal, but I need you now.
God, forgive my limitations, and help me.
Amen.

I had seen several versions of these sentiments before. But never in such a place. Somehow the location and the thoughts went together. A cry from the daily dunghill of existence. Job would have understood.

This plea just about nails down the quandary modern men and women often feel about relating to God or anything godlike. Rational thought takes us just so far. Sometimes we reject every notion we consider. Still, there is this insistent need to relate personally to Something, Sometime, Somewhere. We still have a longing not to feel alienated from ourselves, our world, our universe. A longing for the ultimate reunion—the ritual of reconciliation with God, under exactly those paradoxical conditions found on the door of that toilet.

According to many surveys I have seen, most Americans say, when asked, "Yes, I pray." If you expand the question to include, "Or do you meditate, contemplate, or spend any time in spiritual reflection?" there is an almost unanimous positive response.

Allow me the utilitarian simplicity of saying: Prayer is talking to God. However you may define each of those five words, I'm comfortable. I'll make my circle of understanding as large as need be in order to keep the conversation going. We can get into semantics some other time.

Why do we do this thing we call "praying"?

To worship—to connect in a positive way with the ultimate ground of being.

To confess—to cleanse ourselves of shame, guilt, or remorse.

To thank—to express appreciation for comfort and sustenance.

To petition—to ask for something.

Interestingly, there's not a lot of modern evidence of direct divine response to prayer. Holy books record that God literally spoke in ancient times on many occasions for many reasons. Only about ten percent of those who acknowledge praying say that God has spoken to them. Athletic teams and television evangelists seem to have the most consistent response.

Is there something wrong here? Is this a problem? No.

The responsibility and the opportunity for the relationship belong to the one who prays. God is always there. To put it into scriptural language, "The Kingdom of God is within you."

And the work of that Kingdom is carried out in the human heart.

Prayer is its own reward.

In the ritual of reaching in and in the reaching out.

෴

Another view.

In the realm of Buddhism, prayer takes two complementary forms.

Meditation—the process of inner focusing—of sitting so quietly and silently that the mind is slowly emptied of thoughts and one is not only at the center of one's being but at the center of Being itself.

Action—the achievement of merit by acting in harmony with the best intentions of human community and divine values.

I noticed the intersection of meditation and action in Thailand.

Homage is paid to an image of Buddha by lighting a candle or stick of incense, putting flowers in front of the image, and daily, consciously committing an act of charity to someone in need.

Thais frequently purchase a tiny square of gold leaf and attach it to the image of the Buddha where it will affect the worshiper in a specific way. This is called *"pid tong lung pra."* It is believed that gold leaf pressed on the Buddha's lips will bring the worshiper the gift of eloquence. On the head—wisdom. On the heart—a loving spirit. If the petitioner is ill, the gold leaf is placed on the corresponding area of pain.

It is said that those who have reached a higher level of understanding place the gold leaf on the backside or underneath the image—not for themselves, but for the common good of humanity.

And there are those who say that when one really understands the idea of merit most fully, the money used to purchase gold leaf is instead given directly to someone in need, or placed in an alms box for the temple to disburse.

It is said there is no limit to the amount of good a person can do if he does not mind who gets the credit. This is Enlightenment. This is seeing one's self as an integrated part of the creative forces of life and not just an occasional contributor. The Thais say this is ritual prayer in its highest form—one prays by Being and Doing that which is in harmony with the best interests of all living things.

☙

The reunion with God is often sought in a time of crisis and personal tragedy.

We turn to prayer when we are in need.

Or a time comes when we long to settle our spiritual affairs.

To summarize the character of many conversations with others about this longing, I've constructed an imaginary inner experience:

—

His wife was away for a week.

Alone in bed at night, for no apparent reason, he thought about praying.

He had not prayed in years.

One night, as he was drifting off into sleep, the image of the way he went to bed as a child unexpectedly returned to him. He remembered. With his mother watching from the doorway, he had nightly knelt beside his bed. In his Hopalong Cassidy pajamas, he clasped his hands, closed his eyes, bowed his head, and prayed:

Now I lay me down to sleep; I pray the Lord my
    soul to keep.
Four corners to my bed, Four angels there aspread:
Two to foot and two to head,
And four to carry me when I'm dead.
If any danger come to me, Sweet Jesus Christ
    deliver me.
If I die before I wake, I pray the Lord my soul to
    take.
God bless Mother and Father and everyone and
    everything.
God bless me. Amen.

The part about maybe dying before waking had worried him. So did the angelic pallbearers standing ready to haul him away. It was hard to get to sleep under these conditions.

After he learned the ''Pledge of Allegiance'' in school, he complained to his mother that he didn't like praying aloud anymore. When she agreed he could pray silently to himself, he substituted the ''Pledge of Allegiance'' for his prayer. It made him think of all his friends. Best of all, there was no threat of overnight extinction—nobody died in the ''Pledge of Allegiance.''

When he was old enough to go to bed unsupervised, he gave up bedside prayer. As far as he could tell, nobody else in the family prayed, so why should he? Besides, praying seemed like speaking to a wall. He had talked to God for years. God never talked to him. It was a one-sided conversation. He would wait until God got back to him before he said anything else.

By the time he entered junior high school, the issue of prayer was buried by his busyness. He got involved in school sports and had a morning paper route. He was too occupied to appear at family mealtimes, so he didn't have to worry about saying grace at meals. In fact, the rest of the family was seldom around for mealtimes, either. Father and mother left early and came home late from running the family store. Meals became quick and convenient. No time for grace—not even the quick and convenient sort.

Still, he attended church, mostly for social reasons—to be with friends, to date nice girls. But the hymns and prayers and sermons happened outside of him. Church was another day of school—only on

Sunday. Most of what was said and done in church passed over him, not through him.

There was one crazy, desperate time when he tried to make a deal with God. He had taken his father's pickup truck without permission, driven far out in the country with a girlfriend to find some secluded spot where they could park and neck. She had also broken her family rules by going out with him on a weeknight. About the time they realized how late it was, they also noticed the gas-tank needle on the dashboard gauge pointed to Empty. They were in trouble. Big Time. If what they feared came true, they would be stranded out there in the boondocks, perhaps triggering a search by the Sheriff's Department, and they'd certainly be punished. Their families would throw the book at them: lying, stealing the truck, going out on a school night, being in a strange place doing evil things, annoying the sheriff, making the parents look bad, and adding one more log to the you're-driving-us-crazy fire they had kept burning in their parents' brains for some time now.

So he turned to prayer. Asking God to get them home without any trouble, and if He did, he would never doubt His existence again, and at the next Sunday-evening church service he would walk the aisle in penitence when the call for sinners to reconsecrate their lives to the Lord was made.

He was desperate. If there was ever a call for a miracle in his life, this was it.

And a miracle was exactly what he got. Not only

did the truck make it all the way back, apparently running on fumes, but at both her house and his the parents were elsewhere—themselves out late for an evening. He and his girlfriend got home absolutely free.

Which meant, of course, that not only did God exist, God answered prayer. He didn't know which was a more devastating turn of events—to have been caught by his parents or dealt a bargain hand by God Almighty.

He did his penance. But he wasn't happy about it. And the whole thing confused him. What kind of God was God who could fill gas tanks and manipulate parents when a teenager had done something he knew was wrong in the first place? Maybe he had contacted the Devil instead. His mother said he was going to the Devil. Was this how it worked? He had picked up the phone—but who was on the other end of the line? Maybe nobody. Maybe he was just lucky. Having talked himself out of the corner he was in, he quit going to church altogether. He was beginning to think that more trouble comes from answered prayer than unanswered.

Through college he led a high-speed life. Neither he nor his friends could be described as religious in those years. Prayer was a dead issue. To pray at bedtime or say grace at meals would have seemed most uncool. The only religious event he recalled from his college years was when a fraternity brother reported seeing God during a drunken weekend, but nobody took him seriously. The Devil was still at work.

When he married and had children, the habit of prayers never quite got established in the home. He and his wife talked about it a few times, and both agreed it would be a good thing for the children. Neither one of them took the lead, however, and, like other good intentions, family prayer faded from conscious concern.

During most of his adult life, he only had to deal with prayer at political events or service-club luncheons. How he hated the pontifical braying of men who prayed in public. How finite God must be if He needed these pious yahoos to explain the needs of the world to Him. He figured God didn't need to be informed about anything, least of all the ambitions of businessmen and politicians.

The aversion had lived within him for decades. But now at age fifty, to his surprise, he felt an irresistible urge to pray. It made him uncomfortable. Made him feel vulnerable. How stupid he would feel to be caught on his knees alongside his bed like a small boy. Though he and his second wife talked pretty easily about sex or money or politics, he had never even mentioned prayer to her. He couldn't bring himself to ask if she prayed. And he couldn't figure out why.

Still. Still, increasingly, he felt like praying.

He turned it over and over in his mind.

He wondered if correct posture really made any

difference. He knew that prayer posture varied from religion to religion. Catholics got down on their knees. Muslims got down on their knees and then prostrated themselves. Buddhists sat with legs crossed in the lotus position, hands open on their knees. The Russian Orthodox stood. And the Dervishes and Native Americans danced their prayers. Others poured water over themselves or beat themselves with whips. The Bible suggested one get into a closet and pray in solitude instead of aloud in public.

None of these called to him.

What was *he* supposed to do?

—

One night during the week when he was home alone, he decided to at least try getting in a good frame of mind before going to bed—to go to bed gracefully, for a change, neither rushing at it to meet an arbitrary bedtime deadline nor numbly stumbling into it.

First he changed the sheets on the bed.

Then he lit a candle and placed it in a holder in the bathroom.

From the linen closet, he fetched a towel and washcloth usually reserved for company and opened a fresh cake of lemon-scented soap, likewise meant for guests. It was OK. Tonight he was his own guest.

After a shower, he brushed his teeth, combed his hair, and put on fresh, clean pajamas and his favorite bathrobe.

Walking through the house to his bed carrying the

candle, he felt like a priest in some solemn vespers ceremony.

—

Getting down on his knees by the bed didn't appeal to him at all.

He settled on getting into bed, getting all squared away for sleep by lying on his back with his eyes closed and his hands clasped across his chest.

His mind began to wander.

He considered saying the prayers of childhood, even the "Pledge of Allegiance," but that was nostalgia for then, not prayer for now.

Instead, he thought about the day just passed— what was good in it, which he held on to, and what wasn't, which he let go. It seemed he might just pray a summary "Yes" and "No," affirming all that was right, rejecting all that was wrong.

He thought about his life and considered how long he might live.

He thought about his wife, her face, their love, the sweet pain of her absence.

He thought about his family, those alive and all those long gone.

He thought about his country, seeing it from above—sea to shining sea.

An image of the earth floated up into his mind's eye—in a photograph taken by the astronauts from the moon—this mottled blue-and-green-and-white ball hanging in black space—the earth rising from the moon's surface just as the moon rose on earth.

He thought about Saturn, the stars in the Pleiades, and the Andromeda nebula, and all the bright pinwheels of galaxies out there almost beyond his imagination.

He thought about light and the best title of any book he had ever read, *The Unbearable Lightness of Being.*

Soon he lapsed into nonwords—just feelings, being quiet in his mind.

He imagined he was leaving his body and standing outside himself, looking down at the man in the bed who was somehow trying to pray.

He imagined he was going off to see God. And the last thing he remembered thinking was, ''If I die before I wake, how would I ever know or care? Amen.''

And he slept through till morning.

When he checked the mirror in the bathroom, he was still there.

Propositions—continued:

Rituals are timed by beats of the heart, not ticks of the clock.
Most of our major holidays are connected to seasons.
They are flexible feast days adapted to human needs.
Heart time is not clock time—rituals should never be hurried.

Rituals are frames around the mirrors of the moment.
Rituals are the coin by which attention is paid to the moment.
Nobody lives without rituals. Rituals do not live without somebody.

The function of ritual is paradoxical: to both anchor us to high places on the steep slopes of this world on which we are always losing our footing and to free us from the despair of being stuck in the world's mud.
Ritual behavior softens the phases of life when we are reminded how hard it is to be human. Ritual behavior enriches the phases of life when we are reminded how fine it is to be human.

Is this so?

UNION

Marriages are not as they are made,
but as they turn out.

ITALIAN PROVERB

We know more about weddings than any other public celebration.

You may not be particularly interested in a wedding just now—especially if you haven't been directly involved in one for some time and are not
likely to be anytime soon. Bear with me. I'm using a
wedding as a reference story because it's a common
cultural event—a structure on which I can display
many aspects of rituals.

Above all, I'm using the story to illustrate how all
rituals get re-formed.

This wedding story is not primarily about the half-
hour ceremony contained in a prayer book and performed in a church or synagogue. It's about the
process of making our public celebrations an authentic reflection of our intentions and feelings. If the
best of rituals arise out of real lives, then the real
lives must be considered before the ritual can be assessed.

To avoid confusion for you and the invasion of the
privacy of others, I tell you now that this wedding
story is a combination of three celebrations. Names
and places have been changed, but the rest of it is

true—it all happened, just not at the same place and time. And the people are real, too—but they all weren't at the same wedding.

What is essential to see in the account that follows is that the outcome of the story as I've told it is *truly possible*—not just for weddings, but in human affairs of all kinds.

Come to the wedding—you're invited.

Mary Carrie Goldman and Jonathan Carlos McCarthy

with great joy call upon you to be a witness at their wedding

and invite you to attend the occasion of celebration.

Saturday afternoon at four, the twenty-first day of June, 1993

Fairview Community Center

Columbus, Ohio

Reception and dancing to follow

rsvp

As the guests arrived at the community center around four o'clock, they were directed to the ivy-covered social hall, where high tea was being served. Finger sandwiches and three kinds of tea. An accordionist was playing love songs; several people asked him to be sure and do "As Time Goes By" and "Always" and "It Had to Be You."

Tea, music, and some time. Nice. The guests seemed to be at ease with this opportunity to say hello to people they knew and to be introduced to those they didn't know. At so many weddings you go to nowadays, you don't know who's who or what's what.

After everyone arrived, the minister came in, dressed in his black gown. To gain attention, he rang a little brass bell. On behalf of the bride and groom and their families, he welcomed one and all.

He gave a brief description of the wedding service and then asked the guests to rehearse their spoken parts—saying, in unison, "We do," in answer to being asked early in the service: "Do all those assembled affirm this marriage and give it your blessing?" And he rehearsed them in saying together, "We, your family and friends, now pronounce you married"—to be used near the end of the service. Finally, he led a short practice at applauding and cheering, noting that the guests should not be shy about expressing joy and approval at appropriate places in the ceremony.

Being informed and included in this way put the

guests in an enthusiastic wedding mood. Inclusion is an essential ingredient in a great wedding.

–

The minister presented the groom, Jon McCarthy, who in turn introduced his mom and dad, his stepmother and stepfather, his grandmother, his sister and her husband, and his closest lifetime friend—all of whom were welcomed with proper applause.

The minister presented the bride, Mary Carrie Goldman, who intended to introduce her immediate family but instead choked up with emotion. As did most of the rest of the guests. One little catch in the throat can trigger all the feelings people bring with them to sentimental occasions. The minister observed that tears are right for weddings, and that we all bring deep feelings to such an occasion. Acting on these feelings is appropriate and welcome.

The bride's father, sensing his daughter's need, put his arm around her and picked up the task where she left off, introducing himself and his second wife, noting that the bride's mother had passed away but that he and the bride were pleased to have his wife take a special part in the ceremony. When he spoke the name of his first wife, the father of the bride choked up—as did the rest of us, again. By now quite a few handkerchiefs and tissues were in use. The bride laughed, wiped her eyes, blew her nose, took a deep breath, recovered her composure, and introduced her two brothers, her maternal grandfather, a great-aunt, and her closest lifetime friend.

The minister invited the guests to follow him across the lawn into the main hall, find a place to sit, but remain standing. He urged them to select seats as close to the front of the room as possible, including the front row, to be able to see and hear and be participants in the service, not just spectators. He said, "Don't sit back and watch us—be *with* us."

გთ

With the minister leading and the accordionist playing an upbeat version of "Pomp and Circumstance," the guests moved into the hall and took their places. We were ready.

Here comes the groom!

Down the aisle with enthusiasm, escorted by his grandmother, who had his arm firmly in hers.

Behind them came his mother and stepfather, then his father and stepmother and the rest of his immediate family. They took their places on the minister's left, with the groom standing between his mom and dad.

At a nod from the minister, the pianist played a lovely, lyrical tune composed for the ceremony by a longtime family friend who is a professor of music. The song was like musical candle-smoke drifting in the air.

And, as if carried by the music, quietly, slowly, here comes the bride.

In a bright yellow watered-silk ankle-length dress, with a crown of daisies in her hair. With her dad on one arm and her stepmother on the other, and the rest of her family walking just behind. They stood together on the minister's right, with the bride still linked arm in arm with her parents.

A silent pause, some deep sighs, nervous smiles. Ready.

The minister, addressing everyone, said:

Let your presence be welcome—your hearts be glad.
For everything there is a season,
And a time and purpose for every matter under heaven.
And this is the time and this is the place to celebrate the wedding of Mary Carrie Goldman and Jonathan Carlos McCarthy.
We have come to do all those things, old and new, appropriate to such an occasion.
To say solemn words, to confirm a covenant;
To recognize in this event the place of family, friends, and the human community;
To praise God and the holy spirit of this life;
To laugh and cry, to sing and feast and dance.
Above all, to rejoice in love and its possibilities.

(The minister motioned for us to be seated.)

–

Turning to the parents of the groom, the minister said:

Ian McCarthy and Maria Carlos, you stood in a

place such as this in San Diego, California, on De-
cember 26, 1960, and made a covenant with one an-
other, while wondering in your hearts what would
come of your life together. Part of that answer stands
here between you now—in this man you call "son."

I know the pride you take in him, and the love and
respect you have for him he also feels for you. No
small part of the reason Mary Carrie chooses him
for her husband is all that is you that lives in him—
all that you have given to his life from birth unto
this day.

Jonathan and Mary Carrie bless you for your part
in their marriage.

May we have your blessing on this occasion?

The father of the groom replied:

Mary Carrie, on behalf of the McCarthy family, I
welcome you with all my heart and bless your mar-
riage.

Turning to the family of the bride, the minister
said:

Abraham Goldman, you and Carrie Edwards
stood in a place such as this in Cambridge, Massa-
chusetts, on June 5, 1961, and made a covenant with
one another and wondered what would become of
you and your marriage. Part of that answer is this
woman you call "daughter" who stands beside you
now. I know that the pride you take in her, and the
love and respect you have for her, she also feels for
you. And feels for Louise Rainbolt, who became a
mother to her when Carrie died and you remarried.

No small part of the reason Jonathan chooses Mary Carrie for his wife is because of all that her parents have given to her out of their lives.

Jonathan and Mary Carrie bless you for your part in their marriage.

May we have your blessing on this occasion?

The bride's stepmother replied:

Jonathan, on behalf of Mary's mother, Abe and I and all the Goldman family welcome you and bless your marriage.

The minister stepped forward and addressed the congregation:

You have been called to be witnesses to this wedding because of your friendship and your special relationships to the bride and groom and their families.

I ask if you affirm this marriage and give it your blessing?

The congregation surprised the minister and themselves by shouting back:

We do!

Turning to the bride and groom, the minister invited them:

Jonathan and Mary, come now—stand together here to make your vows.

You have known each other for three years, through the first glance of acquaintance to this moment of commitment. At some moment you decided to marry (and in this case, I believe, it was the bride who asked the groom).

From that moment of yes until this moment of Yes, indeed, you have been making promises and agreements in an informal way. All those conversations that were held riding in a car or over a meal or on long walks—all those sentences that began with "When we're married" and continued with "I will and you will and we will"—those late-night talks that included "someday" and "somehow" and "maybe"—and all those promises that are unspoken matters of the heart. All these common things, and more, are the real process of wedding.

The symbolic vows you are about to make are a way of saying to one another, "You know all those things we've promised and hoped and dreamed— well, I meant it all, every word."

Catch hands now and face one another to make your vows.

Look at one another—remember this moment in time.

Before this moment you have been many things to one another—acquaintance, friend, companion, lover, dancing partner, and even teacher, for you have learned much from one another in these last three years. Now you shall say a few words that take you across a threshold of life, and things will never be quite the same between you. For after these vows you shall say to the world,

This—is my husband. This—is my wife.

Jonathan, please carefully repeat after me:

I, Jonathan, do take you, Mary Carrie,
To be the wife of my days / the companion of my
* house /*
The friend of my life / and the mother of our
* children /*
We shall bear together / whatever trouble and
* sorrow / life may lay upon us /*
And we shall share together / whatever good and
* joyful things / life may bring us /*
With these words / and all the words of my
* heart / I marry you / and bind my life to yours.*

(The groom lost his composure in the middle of his vows and found it difficult to speak, as tears welled in his eyes. The minister put a hand on his shoulder, and the bride put her arms around her struggling husband-to-be and then wiped his tears with her handkerchief. As the groom finished his vows in a whisper, the bride held him tenderly in her arms and hugged him.)

There was a pause while everyone smiled and laughed a little, cleared throats, mustered hankies and fresh tissues and regrouped.

The minister continued:

Mary Carrie, please carefully repeat after me:

I, Mary Carrie, do take you, Jonathan,
To be the husband of my days / the companion of
* my house /*

The friend of my life / and the father of our
   children /
We shall bear together / whatever trouble and
   sorrow / life may lay upon us /
And we shall share together / all the good and
   joyful things / life may bring us /
With these words / and all the words of my
   heart / I marry you / and bind my life to yours.

(Perhaps the bride had never seen her strong, hearty husband so solemn or emotionally undone. Those standing closest to the event would later say that as she repeated her vows, he did truly look as though his dog had died. This must have been what undid the bride, for she began to smile and then giggle as she said the words, and by the time she finished the last phrase, she laughed out loud and threw her arms around her suffering groom and kissed him all over his face. And he laughed. And the minister laughed. And the congregation cheered—at the wrong time as far as the official service was concerned, but as for real life, it was a grand moment.)

When things settled down, the bride was still kissing the groom.

The minister tapped the bride on the arm, saying:

Excuse me, but we really should get on with the service.

Laughter again.

May I have the rings, please.

(The bride's and groom's best friends stepped out

from among the families and stood beside the minister, rings in hand.)

For several thousand years, men and women have exchanged rings as a token of their wedding vows. These simple gold bands are not of great value in and of themselves. But what they stand for now and what they will come to mean over time is beyond price. The great circle of Life itself is symbolized in these small circles on your fingers.

The minister presented the bride's ring to the groom, saying:

Jonathan, place this ring on Mary's finger and
repeat after me:
Mary, I place this ring on your finger /
as a seal on the covenant I have made with you.

(His confidence restored, the groom slipped the ring firmly onto the bride's finger with solemn care.)

The minister presented the groom's ring to the bride, saying:

Mary Carrie, place this ring on Jonathan's finger
and repeat after me:
Jonathan, I place this ring on your finger /
as a seal on the covenant I have made with you.

(The ring did not go on easily at first, but with some struggle the bride and groom together forced it over his knuckle—the minister commenting that a close fit is a good omen.)

The minister then asked: *What other tokens do you have?*

The groom's father came forward with a black in-

strument case and opened it before passing it to Jonathan, who said to Mary Carrie:

*I told you once that I wanted us to help each other
grow and learn. You said you've always wanted to
learn to play the flute but never had the time. I give
you this flute, and I give you lessons and the time to
practice. Make music for us.*

Mary Carrie took the flute, thanking Jonathan with
an embrace.

Then she said to him:

*My family and I want to place in your care some-
thing we've had for three generations—something
just about every member of our family has used since
my great-great-grandfather made it with his own
hands for his first child.*

Mary's grandfather came forward carrying an old
cradle. The audience erupted in applause and laughter. As the grandfather handed the cradle to Jonathan,
he declared in a voice loud enough for everyone to
hear, *"Fill it up."*

Applause and cheers yet again.

The minister spoke to the congregation, explaining:

*I ask each couple who wish to marry to bring a
symbolic meal to this occasion—to remind them that
in the same sense that their bodies need to be nur-
tured daily, so does their love.*

*I ask that they bring whatever is bread and wine to
them, but it must be the real thing—their daily bread,
no matter what it may be: toast, croissants, dough-*

nuts, bagels, ice-cream cones, or bran flakes—whatever they are most likely to eat each day.

I ask them to bring their celebratory drink—whatever they will use to toast each other on their first anniversary and on all important occasions: fine wine, champagne, beer, water, milk—whatever—the real thing. As a sign that for health and love, we do not live by bread alone.

I ask them to bring a plate for the daily bread and either one cup or two, as they choose. These utensils should be ones that either already have meaning for them or will become sacred to them by virtue of being used in this ceremony.

The choices the couple makes say much about their values.

On this occasion, Jonathan has provided a plate from his grandmother's kitchen. On it are two pieces of cinnamon toast—because while both Jonathan and Mary like cinnamon toast best of all for breakfast, they do not agree on just how cinnamon toast should be made. Wheat toast and lots of brown sugar for Mary Carrie, and egg bread with lots of butter and white sugar for Jonathan. They compromised by bringing both styles. (Jonathan's father carried the plate of toast from where it was sitting on a side table to the couple.)

To the bride and groom: Take a small piece of the toast and feed one another that you may be reminded of your responsibility to nurture one another daily, and that you may recognize and celebrate your dif-

ferences. Take a taste from each other's style of cin-namon toast.

(With humorous awkwardness, they fed one another. Too big a piece to eat in one bite—much chewing, crumbs down the front of the bride's gown.)

Minister: *Many days will you share meals at the same table. From time to time, as you eat your daily bread, may you realize that the cinnamon toast has been sanctified by this ritual sharing—may it bring back memories of this day and the vows you have made.*

There are two cups here. One is a pewter beer stein engraved with the couple's initials and today's date, bought by Mary Carrie and filled with beer brewed at home in his basement by Mary Carrie's dad. (Her dad brought the stein from the side table to the couple.)

The other is a wineglass Jonathan bought from the restaurant where you were having dinner the night that marriage was proposed and accepted. You were drinking fancy French sparkling water, so Jonathan bought a case of the water to keep for special occasions. He has labeled the bottles with such dates as First Anniversary, Fiftieth Anniversary, Children, Christenings, Graduations, and Miscellaneous Great Days. (Jonathan's mom brought a bottle of the water, and Mary's stepmother carried the wineglass from the table to Mary and Jonathan.)

Minister: *Drink to one another.* (The bride and

groom take turns giving each other a sip from the stein and the wineglass.)

As long as you live, may you never be too busy to celebrate whatever great occasions come to your lives. May you have many reasons to drink from these vessels.

Will the congregation please rise.

Jonathan and Mary Carrie, before this service you signed the legal papers. You have made vows, exchanged rings, and shared a symbolic meal. On behalf of the state of Ohio, and the religious community that I serve, what you desire has come to pass.

I ask those assembled to join me in this pronouncement, saying together:

"We, your family and friends, now pronounce you married!"

The bride and groom embraced and kissed with such intensity and passion, we should have considered bringing in a privacy screen for this part of the service. They were very good at kissing.

The congregation needed no cue. They had really become accomplished in their part of applauding and cheering at the right moments, and this was a very right moment, indeed. KAFOOM—it was the Fourth of July inside the hall. YAHOOO!

Minister: *Come—let us make a blessing and benediction.* (The immediate family stood around the minister and couple in a circle.)

The minister held out his hand, and the bride

placed a hand on his, followed by the groom's on top of hers, bride's again, groom's again, and minister's on top.

Let us pray together, silently.

(There was quiet for a time.)

Minister: *If a wedding is supposed to be joyful, then we have achieved that and more, I think. The spirit of joy here is one blessing of many.*

Another blessing is this circle of family standing around you, their lives intertwined with yours.

Yet another blessing is all these friends who have witnessed this wedding on behalf of the larger human community.

More than this, Jonathan and Mary, may God bless and keep you;

May the sun of many days and years shine upon you;

May the love you have for one another grow and hold you close;

May the good true light within you guide your way on together;

May your dreams come true, and when they don't, may new dreams arise.

And long, long years from now, may you look at one another and be able to say, "Because of you, I have lived the life I always wanted to live—because of you I have become the person I longed to be."

God bless, God bless, God bless.

Let the music and feasting and dancing begin!

The congregation whoopied all over again.

HOORAY! YES! SIC 'EM, DAWG!

The bride and groom did not march down the aisle.

Marching was not called for. Dancing was.

When the accordionist struck up an old, slow waltz, the groom held up his arms in the dancing position, the bride stepped into his encircling arms, and they waltzed carefully, gracefully down the aisle and out the door and into the rest of their lives.

ͽ∾

(Pause.)

ͽ∾

You might want to take a break here.

Most of those of us at the wedding felt we needed one.

We went to the reception, where we feasted, danced, and more-than-moderately rejoiced into the evening. We went home with reluctance, drained of emotion and satisfied with having played our part in a memorable rite of passage.

What a time we had!

In the days that followed, we talked about why the wedding worked.

When you are ready to take up the consideration of this celebration, I'll take you backstage, and we'll have show-and-tell. Make no mistake, despite its apparent success, there was a struggle backstage. When ceremonies are made out of real lives and not manu-

Certificate of Marriage Registration

This Is To Certify That ....Mary Carrie Goldman...

residing at ....118 Boyd Avenue   Columbus, Ohio...................

born on ....May 9, 1964.......... at ...Cambridge, Massachusetts.......

and ....Jonathan Carlos McCarthy.....................................

residing at........118 Boyd Avenue   Columbus, Ohio...............

born on ....Nov. 5, 1962............. at ......San Diego, California..........

Were Married

date ....June 21, 1993............ at ..Fairview Community Center......
Columbus, Ohio

as shown by the duly registered license and certificate of marriage of said persons on file in this office.

CERTIFIED THIS DATE AT THE CITY CLERK'S OFFICE

date ....July 6, 1993........................

by .... County Executive

by .... Deputy als, the pull-and-push struggle is inevitable. The backstage ritual is more important than the show out front.

This review of the wedding is in eight short sections.

TROUBLE

Does it surprise you to know that what you've just witnessed is a second marriage? Much of what gives strength and beauty to this wedding is the fiasco of the bride's and groom's first marriages. They learned something the hard way the first time. And were determined to get it right this time. This is often the case in ritual celebrations. Why should it be any other way?

Lest I be misunderstood, let me make it clear, in no uncertain language, that if you got it right the first time, you are both lucky and to be congratulated. And if you had a traditional, formal white-gown wedding in a traditional setting with a traditional service and it all went well, leaving you with great memories, then you did the right thing for you. That's the heart of my case—you should do what works for you and your family and friends.

Unfortunately, many couples do not succeed in doing so.

The first time, both Mary Carrie and Jon had married college sweethearts in June a week after graduation. Mary described hers as "the classic Barbie Doll royal fairy princess catastrophe." Jonathan didn't have much feeling for his wedding. "The bride and her mom planned it. They paid for it. All I had to do was get a ring, rent tuxes for me and three friends, and show up."

Their experiences of first marriage were also parallel.

Both families were uneasy and unhappy over their children's haste to marry. They felt the couple was too young, immature, and naïve. And sure enough, both first marriages had gone sour from the beginning. Significant changes occurred in each person during their first years out of college, as they pursued adult jobs and careers. They grew further apart rather than closer together.

For Jonathan, having a child right away greatly strained the relationship with his wife. She wasn't ready for children. When Jonathan's wife became pregnant again and had an abortion without first telling him, he went off and bought an expensive sports car for himself without first telling her. The fierce fighting began that finished by ripping apart the already torn fabric of their relationship. On the third anniversary of their wedding, she filed the divorce papers. Happy anniversary.

It was a quieter story for Mary Carrie. "Love died," she said. "Just slowly shriveled up and died. Our marriage became a prune." When her husband confessed he had fallen in love with someone else and wanted out of the marriage, Mary Carrie wasn't mad or hurt. She was relieved. She actually laughed. Not at the news but at recalling the title of a song she had heard the day before, which pretty well summed up her feelings: ''You did not walk out on me—you only beat me to the door.'' The marriage had lasted four years, and they went quietly out the door of wedded blisslessness together with a lot less noise and ceremony than they had made crossing the threshold of the wedding. When they divided up their possessions, there was little argument—neither of them wanted anything that reminded them of the marriage.

⌒⌒

(An aside—thoughts about statistics on marriage and family.)

As a minister for thirty-four years who has officiated at hundreds of weddings, I can tell you that this account by Jon and Mary is all too common. It is far closer to the norm than we care to acknowledge.

More than half of all first marriages end in divorce.

Marriages that fail usually last about three years, and the highest rate of failure is in the first-marriage, under-twenty-eight-years-old age group. And these are the ones who are most likely to do the full show-biz wedding.

More than half of America's children will be

raised in the complicated circumstances of multiple parenting.

Eighty percent of the population is growing up in or near an urban environment, and seventy-five percent of all women and ninety percent of all men work outside and away from the home.

The world of once-upon-a-time is myth.

Mother and Father and Dick and Jane and Spot and Puff don't live together anymore. If they ever did.

As for the prince-and-princess weddings that ignore these facts of life, we all know how happily real royal princesses live ever after their perfect weddings.

Real people should marry in a real world, not the world of make-believe.

As early as possible in the discussion of a wedding, I ask, ''Where are the land mines—in your personal lives and relationship, and in your families?''

Anybody in the family really unhappy about the wedding?

Anybody in the family not speaking?

Any serious problems with religion, money, alcoholism, mental instability, disease, or infirmity?

I ask if the bride is pregnant, if they've been living together, and how the families feel about such things.

Is either set of parents divorced? And if so, what's the climate between the parents? Are there stepparents to consider?

How did the families feel about the first marriage, and what's left over and unresolved from that?

What's the worst thing that could happen?

—

I have *never* officiated at a wedding that didn't have an element of family discord in it somewhere. Never. Just as I have never officiated at a wedding that did not get out of hand in some way—more people involved, more expense, more of something than was expected or desired. And I have rarely met a young, first-time bride and groom whose wedding and marriage plans were grounded in reality.

—

Like life in general, things do get out of hand.
Life is trouble.
There are *always* land mines.
Not only in weddings, but in every other public rite of passage I know about.

UNTROUBLING TROUBLE

I mention these sobering matters not because I wish to address them in detail here, but because they were part of the consciousness of Mary and Jonathan when they came to see me, and matters of concern from the very outset of our conversations. "We don't want it to be that way again for us—not the wedding, not the marriage, not the family life."

They were eager that their wedding come in the

context of the facts of their lives *now*. They wanted to do everything they could do to improve the odds for a meaningful, workable, satisfactory marriage. They knew what could go wrong. They knew where the big land mines were. They knew that weddings and marriage and life were all bittersweet affairs.

Their realistic view of the matters of marriage kindled enthusiasm in my own heart. I could really get involved in this wedding. I almost hugged them. If I had had a Roman candle and some sparklers in my office that day, I would have fired them off. Hooray for reality!

All progress in human affairs, and there is a great deal, you know, defies the cynics. And though I know it seems hard to believe sometimes, those who learn from experience often profit from their often-expensive education and don't make the same mistake more than twice. The list of what we have learned the easy way is mighty short. Most of us do grow up, and in the growing up, wisdom somehow comes.

There is an essential truth about the rituals of life at stake here. A bedrock-granite kind of truth that should not be missed:

Reformation is essential to vitality in all rituals.

Everything that has life in it must change and grow or die.

The rites and ceremonies marking human events have evolved over time and continue to change, though slowly, slowly. Reformation did not cease with Martin Luther. Re-form-ation is ongoing, led by the needs of live people—and followed, however reluctantly, by organized religion.

The rituals change when the forms of celebration no longer fit our yearnings to celebrate the realities of present circumstances. The rituals change when we reach for a more authentic expression of our deepest human experiences. What does *not* change is the yearning.

This change is nothing new.

It has always been so, is so, and shall ever be so.

It is the nature of life itself, always forming and reforming.

It is neither right nor wrong—it is the way it is.

BIOGRAPHY

You will appreciate their wedding ceremony if you know more about the lives of Jonathan and Mary Carrie. Rituals that have vitality in them arise out of real lives. Rituals that are only words on paper must become flesh and blood or they are empty. Everything's perfect on paper. In real life, it rains on weddings.

Jonathan is a first child, with one younger sister. He had first married at twenty-two, divorced at twenty-five, and was now thirty-one. He has a seven-year-old daughter from that first marriage—she lives with her mother and stepfather in another city. After

Jonathan's divorce, he had dated often, had two semi-serious relationships, and had moved to a new city—Columbus, Ohio—to find a job and attend graduate school for a master's degree in science. In the meantime, both his mother and father also divorced and remarried. The mirror of his family life was cracked, chipped, and broken.

—

Mary Carrie, twenty-nine, is a middle child between two brothers, both close to her in age. She also had married at twenty-two. Divorced at twenty-six. She likewise moved to Columbus, enrolling in the same graduate school as Jonathan.

They met when he accidentally locked her bicycle to his with a cable chain. Waiting around for the "stupid S.O.B." who immobilized her transportation, she forgot her "kick his butt" speech when he showed up and her "heart went pitty-pat." A most unexpected and disconcerting response.

But Mary Carrie had had enough of "that pitty-pat jazz," and politely accepted Jonathan's politely extended apology and rode off on her bike. She didn't see him again for two weeks. But she thought about him. A lot. She didn't see his bike around, either. But she did look a couple of times. Well, maybe every day. It bothered her to have him on her mind, especially when she'd only spent a couple of minutes with him and hadn't really looked at him all that closely.

Her Jewish grandfather used to say, "A man

should smell right,'' meaning she should not ignore her intuition. Also, she had read somewhere that what really attracted people was a chemical substance called pheromones—the molecular essence of a person's scent—literally attracting at the almost subconscious level of smell. She didn't trust family voodoo or spook science any more than she trusted pitty-pat. She had vowed if she ever, *ever* got married again, she would trust her brain. It would be an arranged marriage where she did the arranging— with a man who made sense to her. And then she'd worry about falling in love with him.

So when she found her bike locked to his again, she thought seriously about abandoning the bike and running for her life. But she didn't.

For a long time afterward, Jonathan tried to plead the Fifth Amendment on whether or not he had deliberately locked his bike to hers the second time. He insisted it was a coincidence within the range of statistical probability. She knows now that Jonathan is an incurable romantic. But he's also very good about hiding his feelings and cautious about expressing them.

Despite all her teasing and probing, she didn't get the truth out of him on this subject until the day after she proposed marriage to him. (Don't miss that: *She* proposed to *him.*) In response he gave her the lock and chain he used to shackle their bikes together, along with the combination to the lock. She accepted

ROBERT FULGHUM · 159

it as an engagement ring and still keeps it in a special box in her dresser drawer.

—

They dated for about a year and a half, spending two summers apart. And in that time, as they unfolded their lives for one another, their *friendship* grew. I stress that word because they so often emphasized it when they spoke with me. Also, they talked through their previous marriages—every aspect—especially money, sex, and children. They spoke of their mutual determination to get it right next time. If, of course, they ever did it again. Caution ruled their lives still.

That second summer apart was lonely for them both. The loneliness that leads to daily phone calls and frequent long letters. When they came together in the fall and Mary Carrie was looking for a new apartment, Jonathan put a lumpy envelope in her hand and said, ''Think about it.''

Finding the key to his apartment and the key to his car in the envelope didn't really surprise her. What undid her was the note. *''I'm not very good with words, so I'll keep it simple. I love you. Come live with me. You're the best friend I've ever had.''*

Her heart did a kettledrum-level pitty-pat. She could hear it in her ears.

She didn't cry. She bawled. Overwhelmed with joy and fear.

Refraining from rushing to his apartment and tear-ing the door off the hinges in her enthusiasm, she arranged to move in with a friend for a while. She wrote Jonathan a long letter saying she loved him, too, and would keep the keys. But before she moved in, she wanted to visit his parents and her parents together. She wanted to talk about the place of Jonathan's daughter in the scheme of things, and about her own desire to have children. She even wanted to go to a marriage counselor to have some outside expert help them locate the land mines. She wanted as few surprises as possible. She wanted to do as much of the hard work in the beginning as possible.

And she explained to Jonathan that her grandfather had to smell him first.

BEING INCLUSIVE

This is a "mixed marriage." All you have to do is consider the names to guess at least a mix of Jewish, Irish, Hispanic, Catholic, Protestant, East Coast, West Coast, and in-between. The guest list was a mix of old, young, married, single, divorced, straight, gay, Republican, Democrat, atheist, agnostic, and confused.

I don't consider this unique.

It is my experience that most weddings are "mixed marriages."

It is a reflection of our times and our culture. The great mobility of all those who live in this great

melting-pot-mixing-bowl country of ours has pro-
foundly affected our choice of mates and the compo-
sition of the witnesses at our public rituals. When
this is the case, it is a major mistake to ignore it or
not include it in the wedding considerations.

The choice of the Fairview Community Center as
a site for the celebration is one small indication that
the bride and groom wanted to be inclusive—to
make as many people feel comfortable as possible.

Why a mini-reception before the service?

Actually, it's not such a wiggy idea. It's a thoughtful, commonsense way to make a mix of strangers
welcome at a mixed marriage. Or at almost any public celebration of a rite of passage. There are good
reasons. In this case, the family members were scattered across the country, and nobody lived in Ohio.
Friends also were scattered—and the friendships
were made at different stages in the lives of the bride
and groom and their families. Even the parents had
moved, so that neither set lived where their children
had grown up—especially true for Jonathan's family. This is the nature of life in urban America in the
late twentieth century. It needs to be taken into consideration at weddings, funerals, graduations, and
other occasions where we know the gathered group
are strangers to one another.

So, the wedding was held in the city where the
bride and groom lived and had the most recent and
active set of friends and acquaintances. The pre-
reception helped put people at ease and increased the

odds that people would get somewhat acquainted and at least know who the family members were before the ceremony. It was a sound gesture of inclusion, reflecting the desire to be as considerate as possible of people and circumstances.

The bride nailed it when she said, "The first time all I thought about was me, me, me. This time, it's about us—all of us."

Here's the crux of the matter. The mini-reception idea *worked.*

So well, in fact, that I've often urged it be done. It allows for a graceful reception of latecomers (weddings never start on time), gives early and on-time-comers a comfortable social experience, and allows an opportunity of welcome, inclusion, introduction, and establishment of community. The guests went into the social hall as strangers. They headed for the ceremony from the social hall more as a congregation of people united in purpose. They had met, talked, laughed, and applauded—even learned a part. They knew what to expect and knew they were needed. Above all, they knew there would not be a real wedding without them.

Compare this to all the times you attended weddings where all you did was occupy a seat while something you could not see or hear happened a long distance from you. For all it mattered, your place could have been taken by a hundred-pound sack of sand with a smiley face drawn on it. Afterward, you went to the reception, where you waited in a long line to briefly meet people you would never see again, waited in line for food you don't usually eat, and drank cheap champagne to toast a couple whose marriage you would not give even odds on lasting a year. After that you could have danced to music you can't stand, but you went home. It was a little better than a cocktail party. But not much. I'm exaggerating. But not much.

And if you think I'm getting a little pushy about this, you're right.

When public rituals fail, they fail because they were not inclusive in spirit.

The Golden Rule applies most emphatically to public rituals.

TRADITION

About the music. The wedding music. Any "traditional" music.

Having some good information about tradition makes reform easier. Mary Carrie and Jonathan didn't want the traditional wedding music—partly because it had been played at the first wedding for both of them. But they were reluctant to leave out too much tradition—their parents liked the music, and besides, they didn't know what to substitute.

(The music under discussion here is the "Bridal Chorus" from Richard Wagner's 1848 opera *Lohengrin,* and the "Wedding March" from Felix Mendelssohn's 1826 *A Midsummer Night's Dream.* Vernacularly referred to as "Here Comes the Bride," and "There Goes the Bride.")

I explained that they would be relieved to know the usual wedding march and recessional were not church music and had not been in use for very long. Besides, they didn't have to do what Vicky and Fritz had done.

Vicky and Fritz?

The European royal "wedding of the century" on January 25, 1858, matched Princess Victoria, eldest daughter of Britain's Queen Victoria, with Prince Frederick William of Prussia, eldest son of the emperor of Germany.

Princess Victoria selected the music herself.

For one thing, she made good and appropriate choices—credit is due.

For another, she really liked the music.

As did the English, apparently, for in no time at all, nobility and commoners alike were not only marching down aisles to the same tunes but holding wedding ceremonies that imitated as closely as possible the dress, pomp, and circumstance of that royal example.

The marriage of Vicky and Fritz set the standard of their day and ours. By all accounts, it was a pull-out-all-stops humdinger, and we've been doing our best to keep it up to this very day. Just check the bridal fashion magazines (phone-book thick). The so-called classic American Wedding is more or less an imitation of a British middle-class imitation of a princess's royal wedding of 145 years ago. Lady Diana's wedding to Prince Charles and our fascination with it is a modern-day example of the effect Vicky and Fritz's wedding continues to have.

Odd, isn't it, that the most democratic nation on earth should have such interest in royal standards and behavior? By all accounts and polls, the British royal family ranks higher in favor in the United States than in Great Britain.

Interesting, too, that not since the wedding of Elizabeth and Philip has an English royal marriage gone well, despite the glorious weddings televised to all the world. Is there a clue here?

Don't miss this. It is always the case that what we think of as traditional is a case of somebody, somewhere back there in history, deciding the old way didn't work for them, so they came up with something that did. We can do the same thing.

–

The dress. Can't talk about a wedding without talking about "the dress."

Mary Carrie had bought the princess gown the first time around. It was the first thing she did after becoming engaged. The very next day her mom and she went off to try on dresses. Had a couple of huge fights before they agreed on the Cinderella gown-of-gowns—a full meringue—a lacy, pearly, satiny number with veil and train. More time and thought and money went into the bride's outfit than any other

single item connected to the wedding. This is gener-
ally the case.

Veil, underwear, gloves, shoes, and dress-with-
caboose had cost a bundle. She was embarrassed to
mention the actual amount; she couldn't afford it,
and her parents couldn't afford it. Still, they all kept
saying, ''But you only get married once''—and what
would their friends think if they didn't do it right,
etc., etc.

She wore it once—for a total of three hours.

In time, she hated that dress. Really loathed that
dress.

The day she filed her divorce papers, she put the
princess dress in a black plastic garbage bag and
dropped it in a collection box for a rummage sale.

–

And the tuxedo.

Designed by Edward the Prince of Wales as a
practical dinner jacket, and given its American name
after it was first worn at a country club in Tuxedo
Park, New York, in the late 1890s, the tuxedo has
now become required attire for grooms and waiters.

For his first ''happiest day of his life,'' Jonathan
had gone a step further and rented a full formal
morning suit: swallow-tailed coat, striped trousers,
starched shirt and dicky, vest, foulard, suspenders,
black patent-leather shoes, cuff links, and stickpin.
All inspired by Queen Victoria's husband, Prince Albert, and worn by our model, Prince Fritz, at that
''wedding of the century.'' Jonathan even went for

the top hat. The spats and the walking cane seemed a bit much, but they were available.

His best friend told him he looked like Fred Astaire with a thyroid problem. Maybe Fritz-the-Prince felt cool in this getup, but Jonathan felt like a fool—as if he were going to a costume party. But he had no choice. It was what "went with the bride's dress" and the time of day of the wedding, and it was what his bride and her mom wanted, so what-the-hell. Just do it, don't think about it.

It cost him four hundred dollars. And it smelled funny. He wondered how many other guys had worn the stuff before him. The only part of the outfit he owned was the black knee hose, which he later used to play soccer in, and his own boxer shorts, which were not new. He thinks that when that pair of boxer shorts wore out, he used them as a shoe-polishing rag. He's got nothing to show for his four hundred dollars.

—

Amazing. The bride's dress dictating everything else to do with the wedding. How much sense does it make to spend such a substantial amount of money for a dress to wear once? Or for the groom to rent an outfit, when if he bought the outfit he could at least get a job wearing it—as a headwaiter or a butler or a funeral director or a character in a play? Since when must a wedding be a costume ball? The Victorian Age is over.

We dress for "them." You know—"them," the

invisible people who dictate fashion—people we do not know and never see, yet who must approve of our appearance. It's just big business to "them." Still, we dress for "them"—when we should dress for those we know. Mary Carrie got it right the second time. She wanted the groom to help her pick out her dress—she wanted to please him, too. "How shall I look for you?" she asked Jonathan. He said, in his whimsical way, "Like a daffodil."

Wonderful! Yellow and orange and white and green! She had a dress made she could dance in and wear on special occasions. And her shoes were leaf-green leather, with a strap across the arch—real dancing shoes. She didn't want to pretend to be a princess. She wanted to be just who she was—Mary Carrie Goldman, citizen, woman, beloved of Jonathan Carlos McCarthy.

The groom's apparel was another matter. Jonathan is not really a suit-and-tie kind of guy. You can imagine the discussions. White summer tux outfit? No. Yellow or white or orange or green suit to match the bride? No. Pinstripe business suit? No. Naked? No. Hawaiian shirt and Bermuda shorts? No. But what?

The Hawaiian shirt suggestion rang a bell with his father, who had purchased a fine ivory-colored linen suit to wear at his retirement party when he left the navy. He had not worn it since. Somehow it reminded him and Jonathan of how Bogart looked in

Casablanca. A few alterations and it would fit. Yes. His father was pleased. The bride was ecstatic. Yes, indeed! Bring on Bogey!

Jonathan dressed like Bogey? Is there a contradiction here? Of course. Some fantasy always creeps into our celebrations, as well it should.

–

When it came to the ceremony, we spent more time on the single issue of who walked down the aisle with whom and who stood where than anything else in the wedding. This is *always* the case. That seventeen seconds takes weeks to get straight. People know a lot about pecking orders and symmetry, and spend time on what they know about.

The stepparent issue is, was, and always will be a land-mine area.

It was clear that while the parents and their new mates were determined to cooperate and not make trouble, everybody knew very well that there was some old, unsorted garbage lying in the corners. This is likewise true at funerals, graduations, recitals, and all family dress parades.

There were some tense moments as we tried to find solutions. And a State Department protocol expert could not have worked this out to the perfect satisfaction of everyone. There was heavy baggage from the past here that nobody wanted to sort out, but nobody could pretend it wasn't there, either. Jonathan said his mom would like to get her hands on his father one last time, just to leave a few scars. But the mother kept her cool and sat on her hands, at least in public.

It helped to have everyone involved in the problem. It doesn't always happen like this. I could tell you some nasty stories. But it *can* work out—it just takes grown-ups to do it. And sometimes grown-ups show up to do the work.

I emphasize: Being inclusive helps.

The bride and groom walked down the aisle with all their parents to honor their relationship with them. All the parents got at the first weddings was a front-row seat; otherwise, they were spectators. A painful experience for them.

Her father did walk her down the aisle that time and gave her away when asked, but neither he nor Mary Carrie liked it—they did it because they thought they were supposed to. The idea in this day and age of anybody giving anybody away as property to another, male or female, seems absurd. But the idea of having your parents be an important part of your wedding is not. It is a very traditional notion, actually—and a tradition worth keeping.

They walked down the aisle with their parents because they both began to understand that their parents had always been there for them and that their presence should be honored. As Mary Carrie and Jonathan got older, the more they realized the importance of their parents in their lives—and the more they valued family. I observe that this realization always takes time.

There were no matching sets of bridesmaids and groomsmen. If you remember, the bride and groom each asked the closest members of their immediate family to walk with them and stand by them, along with one really close friend. And all were asked to dress up as it pleased them, as it made them feel right. Nobody had to fit a theme, and nobody had to match. Let's get real here: Most human beings do not come in matching sets.

As it turned out, everyone looked just right—not like dukes and duchesses or men-at-arms. They came as who they were—like family, all dressed up for something special. Only the groom's grandmother stood out—she was smashing in a bright pink dress with hat to match. But as I said, everyone looked just right.

"We want to include our families in the actual service somehow. Is that possible?" Of course. Not only possible, but I think it's necessary. Besides, I emphasize that it's a very traditional thing to do. Up until the twelfth century in Europe, a wedding was always a family affair, and in most cultures worldwide it still is. But when the concept of romantic love and chivalry got loose in Western culture, family ties got left out, and the arranged marriage was replaced by love, sweet love. So much so that it is not uncommon for families to meet for the first time the day before the wedding and not ever meet again unless somebody dies.

––

You may have noticed a lack of symmetry in the wedding service. Not everybody said or did the same thing in the same way, even if they had similar roles. This, too, is compatible with long-standing tradition. A Jewish carpenter once noted that "the Sabbath was made for Man, not Man for the Sabbath." And weddings were made for people, not the other way around. People must not be forced to fit the form— the form must fit the participants. When it does not, it must be re-formed.

For example, not only was the bride's stepmother much beloved by Mary Carrie and her father, but Abe is a large, powerful, confident, and terribly sentimental man. Given half a chance, he will turn a ritual line into a long-winded and tearful speech, personally blessing everyone present, in the name of Abraham, Isaac, Jacob, and all the great Jews who ever lived. He admits it. It's a family joke. His second wife is a teacher—confident in public and strict about sticking to the words of the text. It was Abe's idea that she speak for the family, thereby pleasing all.

Notice, in passing, how many opportunities a wedding has for secondary celebration of relationships. A wedding is both a union and a reunion. Consider how many of those involved want and need recognition and affirmation of their place in the life of the bride and groom. Friends, family, even special acquaintances, can be included in ways that will leave you and them more intimately bound together. The part played by Mary's stepmother is a great example.

HUMAN EVENTS

When I meet with the bride and groom the last time, I make a speech:

Weddings are a lot like any other occasion in life. Anything can happen.

The great banana peel of existence is always on the floor somewhere.

Not only that, anything might go right!

Sometimes the unexpected is an unforgettable moment that transforms a standard wedding into a memorable experience. The sweetest memories are seldom the result of planning. Forget fashion shows, forget a performance, forget perfection. Whatever happens gets acknowledged and included. Whatever happens, we work it in.

Nothing can ruin a wedding if the heart is right.

Nothing can help a wedding that is a military drill. Relax.

Be here. Notice each other. You could walk through fire together!

I also advise them to go to the bathroom one last time before they make their public appearance. I am a practical man.

–

And sure enough, the wedding did not go according to plan.

Jonathan surprised everyone, including himself, by choking up with tears in the middle of his vows, but it was also no surprise or violation of protocol for Mary Carrie to wipe his tears and comfort him. It was OK. As was Mary Carrie's laughter during her vows. I'm never sure who is going to do what, but tears and laughter are welcome in a ceremony.

Which is why I always ask someone in the wedding party to carry a couple of handkerchiefs. It's just too embarrassingly funny for a groom to wipe his tears and runny nose on his cuffs.

Amateurs under emotional pressure at great moments often lose their composure and do what people do then—cry, snivel, sneeze, bawl, giggle, yawn, laugh, hiccup, go mute, get sick, pass gas, or pass out. I have been present as the 911 officer when all these things have occurred during weddings. And not only on the part of the bride or groom. I've found that almost anyone present can react in such a fashion—and that sometimes it's catching, especially tears and laughter. And there is extraordinary humor close at hand. Some other time I will tell you in detail about brides in huge dresses getting stuck in small bathrooms.

GIFTS

The earliest evidence of wedding rings dates back to around 2800 B.C.E. in Egypt. Well over 4,000 years ago. In the year 860 the Roman Catholic pope, Nicholas I, decreed that an engagement ring was required of those who agreed to marry. A simple band, preferably of gold, should be given by the man to the woman to wear on her finger, and if either violated the vow to marry, he or she was subject to excommunication, or the woman could be banished to a nunnery for life.

I wonder what Pope Nicholas would have thought of the bicycle chain Jonathan gave to Mary Carrie?

The practice of giving tokens other than rings within the ceremony is also a tradition that goes way back into human history. Anything used or exchanged within the ritual context takes on special meaning—and may become part of the covenant.

Jonathan's gift of a flute, Mary's gift of the family cradle, are just two examples of many I have seen: seven fruit trees—one for each star in the Pleiades; something secret in a small box to be opened on the couple's fiftieth anniversary; a locket containing a picture of the groom and a snip of his hair; a pocket watch; wildflower seeds; a kayak paddle; even a gift certificate for matching tattoos. Who is to say what shall have meaning for others? Who is to say what shall have lasting value?

My own wife didn't want a diamond ring. As a

sentimental joke, I went ahead and bought a simple, stylish ring with a knock-your-socks-off stone. The best stone (glass, actually) that Woolworth's had: $2.98 plus tax. I put it in a box finagled from the best jeweler in Seattle and gave it to her on the day of our wedding. She was nonplussed.

But when I gave her the sales receipt in case she wanted to return it, she all but bowled me over with a laughing embrace. She loves that stupid ring as much as if it were real. And it is real, isn't it?

She wears it now on fancy occasions. People are always impressed. It's hard not to crack up when someone admires her ''diamond.'' We always confess and pass on the story. The story shines. The actual ring is nothing. But when she wears it on her finger, we are bound together by the memory of its meaning, and *that is everything.*

Just recently, her mother gave her a lovely gift. The wedding ring her husband had given her. She had a copy made for herself and gave the original to her daughter. Since I think her folks have a great marriage, I, too, really like seeing my wife wear that old ring—it's a good omen for all four of us.

GOD

''We're worried about God, and worried about praying in the service,'' said Mary when I met with her and Jonathan and both sets of parents. An awkward silence in the room. ''Jonathan and I don't belong to any church in particular, and our parents and friends are a mix of everything. We're still struggling with what we believe. We don't want to offend anybody, but we don't want to say things we don't accept. We want to have the service be as inclusive as possible, without being wishy-washy or patronizing or dishonest.''

The parents were still quiet. Jonathan spoke up. ''Very few people at the wedding will know the same prayers or hymns. It's going to be awkward. And isn't God everywhere all the time? He doesn't need to be sent for or have anything explained to Him, does He?''

The families had openly discussed almost every detail of the wedding. They had been careful not to get too far into religion. Or maybe it wasn't religion they were avoiding, but a complex mix of ingredients stuck to the core of religion: tradition, custom, habit, language, theology, reputation, and desire. And most of this was unexamined—they'd never thought about it much or questioned it; it was too close to their very identity.

Everybody was clearly deeply concerned about how to handle this. And nobody had any enthusiasm for unloading and sorting out the whole freight-car load of religious differences before the wedding. They all looked at me.

–

Here's what I said, and what I believe.

More often than not, it's our metaphors that separate us—our choices of analogies for what cannot be named or spoken or expressed in any correct way in human language.

God, that name we use most commonly for the Ultimate Ground of Being, is everywhere at all times, and though we think of God in many ways, there is nowhere God is not. No matter what is or is not said at a wedding, God is there and may be summoned or experienced within each person there in ways in keeping with their own faith and views and language. This is not a competition.

If the spirit of the wedding is right, then the entire service becomes a prayer for the bride and groom and all their friends and relatives to live in harmony with great and eternal truths.

Furthermore, I perceive that the bride and groom are more religious than they are aware. To walk humbly with thy God, to love thy neighbor as thyself, to do unto others as thou wouldst have others do unto thee—these are the essential foundations of religion. Are these fundamentals present in this couple? Yes.

From all I know of Jonathan and Mary Carrie, I say that they and their wedding plans pass the test. They have drawn the circle as large as they can to include us all. And left room for mystery. What we are going to do is right and good.

–

You will not find the wedding service of Jonathan and Mary Carrie described in any of the great scriptures or canons of any major religion. In fact, there is no wedding service of any kind in any of the great scriptures. Neither the Buddha nor Mohammed nor Jesus wrote a wedding service.

In the Christian Church it wasn't until 1439 at the Council of Florence that the marriage act was sanctified as sacrament, one of the seven channels of grace. Organized religion has revised the wedding form many times. And will continue to do so, I'm sure. People make rituals as we find a way to make rituals meaningful.

If you accept the great scriptures as the Word of God, it would seem that God is not concerned with the actual words spoken as couples cross the threshold into the house of marriage. The concern is for the relationships between those who live out their lives together in that house.

ନ୍ତ

I return to the beginning of this discourse.

Take my advice. Consider this compassionate counsel.

In the matter of weddings or any other major public ritual occasion.

Use your brain as well as your heart.

Know where the land mines are.

Don't step on them if you can help it.

Make rituals serve your lives, not the other way around.

Marching in step isn't required, but, like Jonathan and Mary Carrie, you may choose to waltz across the threshold of any great passage in your life.

BORN

What the child sees, the child does.
What the child does, the child is.

IRISH PROVERB

Foot Prints

Register Your Identity

Age

Left Foot _____ Age 3 Mo. Right Foot

This Certifies that the above foot prints of

Robert _____, Lee _____, Fulghum _____
(First)   (Middle)   (Last Name)

were made in the _____ Baptist Hospital _____
                        (Institution)

Enid _____ Oklahoma _____
(City)   (State)

on the ___4th___ day of ___June___ 19_?_A.D.

by _____
        (Person officiating)

Signed _____
           (Supt. or Physician)

(Father's signature and right hand finger-prints)

Each of us is unique, one of a kind.

And the ritual celebration of the uniqueness of individual existence has taken place as far back in human history as we have records, and probably before. Ritually, we welcome a child into the community, our world, and the universe.

Or at least we used to do this.

There is a change in ritual practices around birth—a substantial change: a lack of celebration. This may be a sign that, as the population grows, so does the distance between us.

Keeping in mind my intention of being useful to those who ask about ritual, I share with you now a service that combines two distinct elements: the welcoming of a child, and the union/reunion celebration of being neighbors.

As with the wedding example, this is a consideration of how we find ways to celebrate by reforming tradition—an example of a process as much as a model of a form. And in doing something contemporary, the parents of the child returned to something very old in human affairs.

As with the wedding example, the sharing is in

two parts: first, the description of the event, followed by a backstage tour.

಄

A child is born!

There is an optimistic ring to that powerful proclamation—even under the worst of circumstances. I have been told that in Europe during World War II families sought refuge from shelling in unfilled open graves in cemeteries. In these graves, women gave birth. As awful as life seemed at the time, when word was passed around the graveyards that ''a child is born!'' hope was mended for a moment in the hearts of those who heard. In the Jewish tradition, any child might be the Messiah, even if born in a graveyard. ''You never can tell . . .'' we say, and ''Who knows what might happen because of this child?'' In every tradition, a child is born of the seed of hope.

Biologically, we are wired to affirm birth. Culturally, we have found countless ways to commemorate the event as if compelled to celebrate by the sheer force of life itself. ''It's a girl!'' or ''You have a son!'' Hooray! Wahoo! Let's party!

My wife, a physician, tells me that the delivery of a healthy baby is a peak experience in the practice of medicine. She says she always has tears in her eyes at the moment a child is born. For all she knows of physiology and biology, birth remains beyond science—an awesome miracle.

"What's it like to deliver a child?" I asked her over supper one night.

She's silent, thinking, but I see her hands automatically respond—one over the other to carefully cradle the emerging head of a child.

"It's a very wonderful kind of scary. These days you pretty well know what to expect because of all the tools and techniques and tests available for monitoring the baby. Still, anything can go wrong.

"At the beginning, there's usually a lot of anxious waiting around, and then gradually the pace picks up. In the final stage, a tiny circle of the top of the child's head appears in the vaginal opening. With each contraction, more of the head appears, until it emerges, facedown, and the baby rotates ninety degrees and you can see its face. Then you use a little pressure to help the shoulders out. After that, the rest of the body usually emerges easily. I always try to find out ahead of time if the parents have a name picked for the child, because I like to call it by name and say as soon as I know, 'It's Jennifer!' or 'It's William!'

"No matter how many times you've been present in the delivery room, there's always that magnificent moment of relief and joy when a healthy baby is born."

Getting born doesn't always happen as smoothly and joyfully as my wife described it. And since everything about us is primed for affirmation, it is no wonder that we feel almost unbearable pain when a

child is miscarried or born deformed or born un-
wanted: the door to the feast hall of joy is closed and
locked. As a Greek friend put it when his child died
at birth, ''I drink now from the cup of sorrow.''

But in this day and age, more often than not, when
a child is born, it is a WOW! occasion. We relay the
joyful news urgently: ''It's a girl!'' ''I'm a father!''
''You have a grandson!''

Given this universal urge of exultation, it is difficult to explain why the formal ritual celebrations of
the birth of a child have diminished in frequency, importance, and size in our time and culture—certainly
in comparison with the major public celebrations of
weddings and funerals. Organized religion has less
and less a part in this passage of life. Though it's
hard to get an accurate figure, my guess is that fewer
than a quarter of the children born these days are celebrated in any kind of formal way. Why?

There are understandable reasons. Cultural mobility, for one.

Since young couples frequently live far away from
immediate family, are not well established in a community, and are not closely connected to an organized religious group, a public celebration of the
birth of a child is not as easily accomplished as it
used to be.

And young parents are more likely to have reser-
vations about infant circumcision, infant baptism or
dedication, or any other rite offered by organized religion.

"Besides," one young mother explained, "who's got time? My husband and I both have jobs with limited parental leave—and the same is true of our friends and neighbors. All my closest family live on the other side of the country. And my husband and I are too overwhelmed just coping with being parents to put together a celebration. If we had any extra time, we'd get some extra sleep, not plan a celebration. I didn't get my first child's birth announcements out until the kid was almost a year old; with my second child, I considered just sending the birth announcements along with his high school graduation invitations."

The most daunting difficulty is excessive and irrational expectation.

There's this social myth that says the celebration of a newborn child should be a well-organized, serious, dress-up occasion, with all the stops pulled out, and if you can't do that, do nothing.

Not so. Not so. And the ritual of welcoming a child need not preclude or substitute for a formal celebration within an organized religious community, now or later, if the family chooses to have one.

The birth of a child is such a big deal in itself that a big deal doesn't have to be made of it for the occasion to be satisfying and memorable. Many of our finest human moments are rather small in scale, but large enough in spirit to last a lifetime.

Especially when a child is born.

—

Ed and Lila Brown write to announce the birth
of our second child,

Maxwell Peterson Brown

and to invite you to a celebration of his birth,
at our home on Sunday afternoon,
May 2, 1992 at three o'clock.

Since Max will be growing up here, we want
him to know his neighbors and his neighbors to
know him from the beginning. Refreshments
followed by a brief service. Please come in your
comfortable Sunday afternoon clothes and bring
some very small, sentimental, token gift of welcome
to be put away in a treasure box and given to Max
when he is twenty–one to connect him to his
beginnings. Perhaps a flower from your yard,
a picture of the neighborhood, or just a note of
hello and good wishes will do – nothing
fancy – as you feel comfortable.

Thanks for coming!

RSVP

Come with me to a celebration of birth—a welcoming of a child.

A pattern repeats itself once more here. As with the wedding ceremony, this celebration works out in a positive and joyful fashion. But pain and anxiety are in it, too. And it is the product of what people do when they've done something that didn't work the first time around and are determined to profit from their experience—determined to increase the odds that something right and memorable will be done this time.

The specifics of the event are not nearly as important as the frame of mind that shaped the celebration. This is true for every successful public ritual.

☺

Suppose you find a hand-delivered envelope in your mailbox.

Inside is an invitation, with a note addressing you by name, saying we really hope you can come.

Imagine you've been invited because you are a neighbor, two houses down, of a young couple who moved to your block about a year ago. The Brown family. You don't know them much beyond a nodding acquaintance and what you've noticed from a distance.

They have one child, one car, and no pets. They keep their yard neat and their car washed. Parents and child leave together early each morning and arrive home together each evening, so the child must be in day care while both parents work outside the home.

During the past year, you noticed the increasingly pregnant condition of the mother. From neighborhood chitchat, you hear that their new child is born. You also hear that the child has a serious heart defect and may need corrective surgery.

You ought to go over and meet them, but, well, it's a little awkward, and somehow you don't get around to it. Neighborhoods aren't the same as they used to be. Time passes. And now you have this invitation.

When you arrive, Ed Brown is there to greet you at the door. You recognize him, but in case you didn't know, he is wearing a bright green apron imprinted with large white letters declaring, ED BROWN—THE DADDY. Ed is short, swarthy, balding early—a mixture of warmth and shyness. "Welcome and thanks so much for being here," he says. "Please come in, make yourself at home—everybody is in the backyard, out through the kitchen."

You walk into the living room where there's the wooden box in which to leave the little gift you've brought—on a table beside a guest book. The table is hosted by a well-dressed older woman—Ed's mom. You know because she is also wearing a green apron: VI BROWN—ED'S MOM—GRANDMA.

After appropriate pleasantries, she points you in the direction of the kitchen door. Outside under the trees, you see chairs and benches, tables with food and drink, and a couple dozen people—about half of whom you recognize as neighbors. It's troubling to realize that while you recognize your neighbors, you do not, in fact, know many of them very well—this will be the first time to socialize with some of them. Well, good—it's about time.

There are more green aprons. EDNA PETERSON— LILA'S MOM—GRANDMA and JOHN PETERSON— UNCLE and JACK BROWN—ED'S DAD—GRANDPA. Staffing the barbecue grill is a lively, laughing man wearing a green apron that says, SI GREEN—CALL ME ANYTIME. You will learn later that Si is a "character," best friend of the father and solely responsible for the special aprons, which may be a little cornball, but they do the job. The aprons help create an open, friendly, welcoming atmosphere.

Off to one side but at the center of attention, sitting in a rocking chair, is Lila, holding her son, Max. Tiny child, wrapped in an ivory-colored blanket, asleep. Redheaded mom, fine-freckled features, flower-print dress.

It's almost too perfect—hard to believe such a time is still possible: a warm afternoon in May, blue skies, flowers, trees, neighbors, friends, family, food, and a newborn child. And nothing to do but just be there. Lovely. We could use more of this. We could make time for more of this.

—

After timelessness has settled in on the gathering—when everyone has a chance to get a nametag, say hello, and have a cup of tea or a glass of lemonade—one of the guests you've met taps a spoon on a glass and asks for attention:

Hello. I'm the master of ceremonies. On behalf of

Ed and Lila, let me emphasize how welcome you are and how much we appreciate your coming and participating.

We used to live across the street from the Browns and have spent a lot of time together, especially on hiking trips. They asked me if I would help them celebrate the birth of their son, Max, and I'm honored to be part of this occasion.

Since there are not a whole lot of us, and some of you have barely become acquainted this afternoon, let's make sure we all know who is who. Will you introduce yourselves and tell us how you fit into the occasion?

The family present include Ed's mom and dad and Lila's mom, her brother, and his wife—all from out of town. Also the principal of Lila's school and her husband, and the neighbors from seven houses close to the Browns'. Si Green, Ed's best friend, who runs Ed's favorite restaurant, has catered the refreshments and takes time to explain about serving food after the service.

A special note about Si. He has not only brought the food and the printed green aprons for the family, he has provided balloons, a bubble machine, and colored streamers. More important, he has brought enthusiasm, laughter, and mischief. Every solemn occasion needs a jester—a sacred clown. It's a very old human tradition to balance the serious with the lighthearted. Here's to all the Si's of this world— bless them all!

The master of ceremonies continues:

To put you at your ease, let me tell you about the service. You've been invited because you are important to the Browns, and you have a part to play in the ceremony.

In a moment, we'll go into the living room, and I'll stand in the middle of the room with Lila and Ed and Max beside me, the immediate family around us in a circle and everyone else in a circle around the family. It's important that everyone be able to see and hear, especially the children present, so we'll take time to arrange ourselves with that in mind—we're in no hurry. Small children can stand on chairs. The service is brief, but if children cry or talk or sing or run around, we'll accommodate them.

At the end of the celebration, I'll ask all of you to join me in a blessing:

"We, your neighbors and friends and family,
bless this child, his parents, and his home.
May God bless us all, Amen."

Let's rehearse that, line by line, so that we do it well when the time comes.

—

After getting our lines right, we go inside and find our places. The master of ceremonies and the parents stand behind a small table bearing the gifts, the large wooden box, a single candle, a vase containing a single red rose, and a small bowl of water.

Smaller children stand on dining-room chairs so they can see. The Browns' daughter, Sarah, aged four, red hair and purple coveralls, sits on a tall stool, mightily alert but supervised by her grandfather Brown, who holds her hand. When everyone is settled, the master of ceremonies says:

> *We have come together on this fine day in May to rejoice in life.*
> *And to welcome life bound up in this child.*
> *We have come to take time to notice one another; to see ourselves in the many ways we affect the life of this child as neighbors, friends, family, and parents.*
> *What name have you given this child?*

Lila looks down for a moment at her child asleep in her arms and says,

"Maxwell Peterson Brown."

And Sarah pipes up to announce, "But we call him Max."

The master of ceremonies, smiling, lights the candle, saying,

> *We light this candle for Maxwell Peterson Brown; may his light shine now, and all the days of his life.*

The master of ceremonies stands close by the mother and child—looking down at the child, he takes the child's right hand in his own and says:

*Well, Max, welcome to this world—this amazing
and scary world.*
*Welcome to light and dark, hot and cold, good
and evil.*
*Welcome to love and hate, truth and lies, good
times and bad.*
*Welcome to the long human pilgrimage from
birth to death.*
*Anything can happen here—everything is
possible.*
*Welcome to the companionship of the human
family.*

Max wakes up and opens his eyes.

The master of ceremonies picks up the small bowl
from the table, saying:

*Your mother and father are pretty sure you were
conceived on a camping trip when rain kept them
cuddled in a tent for the weekend. That's what they
hoped and wanted. Your father filled a canteen from
the rain streaming off the tent and kept it to use to
drink a toast to your mother if she turned out to be
pregnant. Some of that water was saved for this occasion, as well.*

*Water is the most ancient and universal symbol of
life used in every religion as a metaphor of vitality—
for without water there is no life. On behalf of this
community, I place a little of this token of the stream
of life on your forehead.*

He moves close to Max with the ceremonial bowl of water to dip his finger in the water, but Max beats him to it—slapping his tiny fist into the water and splashing himself, his parents, and the family. Sarah laughs, igniting laughter around the room. Before the bowl of water can be moved out of his reach, Max slaps the water again, smiles, gurgles, kicks his feet, and waves his arms. The master of ceremonies wipes his face and says:

Thanks, Max. We came to bless you, and it is you who have blessed us.

He takes the rose from the table and says:

This rose is another ancient symbol of life. With all its beauty, it bears thorns.

One does not come without the other. So with the raising of children.

Ed and Lila, I scatter the petals of this rose over you and Max and place the thorny stem in the memory box so that you and Max might not forget the mix of this life. In this same box go all the gifts from those present, along with letters you have written to your son to be opened on his twenty-first birthday.

This box does not only contain memories. It is filled with hope.

As most of you know, Max has been born with a tiny hole between the chambers of his heart. His existence is somewhat fragile. The good news is that surgeons can repair that hole, and Max may live a long life—if all goes well. In the weeks to come, Max and his family will need your support, your help, and your prayers that Max will endure and take his place with the children growing up in this neighborhood.

Maxwell Peterson Brown: live long, live well.
Know that you belong to yourself and eternal
  God.
Know that you are in the care of all those who
  surround you now.

There is silence in the room. Except for the sounds of Max gurgling.

Please join me in the blessing:

"We, your neighbors and friends and family, bless this child, his parents, and his home. May God bless us all, Amen."

And Sarah pretty well sums it all up by shouting at that moment,
"HOORAY FOR MAXIE!"
After hugs and handshakes, we drift out to the backyard for food and conversation, which go on well into the afternoon. Two guests break out a fiddle and a guitar, playing an up-tempo version of "Amazing Grace," and music drifts across all our lives like invincible summer.
A child is born.
And a child is welcomed.

(And pause again.)

෧෧

As in the case of the wedding story, this birth celebration was discussed by the participants for some
time before and after the occasion. It represents a revival of something very old in human tradition—inviting the neighbors in. And in doing so, providing
connections within the neighborhood that have
lasted.

This welcoming of a child is a useful example of
how ritual can be reformed to fit the present, while
reviving the past and serving the future.

To fully appreciate the ceremony, you need to
know more about the lives and circumstances of the
participants.

Once again, the backstage tour is divided into
small sections.

෧෧

What would you have contributed to the memory box?

I'd like to know the contents of that time capsule. I'd like to be there in 2013 when Max opens his presents and reads his mail. I was there, and I'll tell you my gift. When Ed and Lila and my wife and I were on a backpacking trip in southeastern Utah several years ago, we stopped at a mineral shop along the highway. Some slices of a piece of iron meteorite were for sale. It appealed to me to own something that had once been whirling around in outer space. I really wanted a piece of that meteorite. But it was too expensive for my budget. So Ed bought it for me as a gift.

And that's why it seemed just right to give it to his son. I put that little piece of the sky in a tiny box, along with a note to Max explaining how I was returning his father's generosity along with a piece of advice: ''Always consider the stars.''

As you see, I have a deep and abiding friendship with Ed and Lila. I like who they are and what they do and what they want. He's an attorney, and she's an English teacher. Behind very businesslike, professional surfaces, they're very sentimental, and though they would be uncomfortable admitting it, they're very religious people. They just haven't settled on a way to express it.

Ed was raised a nonpracticing Catholic, and Lila grew up vaguely related to the Lutheran Church, but they dropped their connection to organized religion when they went to college. They don't belong to any church. It's interesting how often matters of philosophy and religion come up in our conversation and how long and hard we've often argued over the precise use and meaning of words, especially when it comes to matters of philosophy or religion.

This rational free-for-all over religious language is a mask for Ed and Lila's uncertainty about their unspoken longing for meaning. I see them protecting their feelings because they're vulnerable when it comes to emotional matters. They yearn to express their deepest human concerns, but they're afraid of feeling awkward or hypocritical. I see all this as a good sign—their struggle will in time lead to a spiritual homecoming. In the meantime, shall life be put on hold? I think not. If they know the road they are on is the right one, it doesn't matter if they don't hurry along it at high speed.

When Max was born, they were ready to "do something." Something they missed doing when their first child was born. At that time, Ed was in the air force paying off his obligations from graduate school, on temporary duty in Japan—far from family and friends. Their life was too hectic then to do much more than cope with the first child. But they felt something missing—some ritual celebration that should have happened but didn't.

When life settled down and Sarah grew from baby

to little girl, they felt this need for ritual on a daily basis, so they had started holding hands with her at mealtimes—with eyes closed and heads bowed in silence, ending in "Amen." They liked doing that, though they had not yet found words to say in this family setting or a way to say grace when they had friends to dinner.

Long before Max was born, they began informally talking to me about what might be done to welcome him—and where and how. How about doing something very privately—with just me present? No. That wasn't enough. They needed other people somehow. How about joining a group of parents for the welcoming-of-children service at my church? No, too much—not ready for that.

Whatever they did it had to be honest, authentic, lucid, and real. I asked them to tell me how they would like to feel a week after the event. "Connected," they said—to whatever God is, to life, to each other, to friends, family—to something bigger than themselves. And they wanted to feel good about their ability to step off the treadmill of life and give its stages meaning.

It was interesting to see words fail two people who make their living from their expertise with words. But understandable. I knew what they wanted and that words could only point at it—words could only acknowledge what could not be spoken. There's no magic in the words or ceremony. Only the inner thoughts and feelings for which a ritual stands give it meaning. As is often the case, keeping the ceremony simple and human is the best way.

DETAILS

The service for Max speaks for itself. And it worked. It had the comfortable feeling that comes when ritual is not forced or faked.

Every part of it was carefully considered. We first made a pile of all the ideas about what might be done, suspending judgment until we had thought of every reasonable possibility. As with premarital conversations, this talking was part of the celebration and not just a rehearsal for the ceremony. Finally, we cut away everything that seemed forced or redundant or unnecessary.

A few items might well bear a little explanation. I'd like to emphasize the importance of what may seem minor matters, and avoid some misunderstanding about what are major considerations.

–

The service was short for practical considerations as well as spiritual ones—to allow for the attention span of children, for one thing, but also because a lot of words aren't necessary at these times. Everyone there brought feelings, thoughts, and experiences to bear on the celebration—and considered them within themselves as we stood together. We knew why we were there. Even the children would know—if they were respected—and the language was directed at them.

This is true for every public ritual occasion.

If children are present, children should be considered and included.

Children should be present at a welcoming ceremony. And accommodated.

Adults should acknowledge that sometimes children will cry or talk or even throw a fit on such occasions and plan for it. This is why Grandpa Brown was charged with paying attention to Sarah—and if Sarah needed to be held or hugged or addressed or distracted or taken to the bathroom, the ceremony would be adjusted.

Likewise, Max was kept in the arms of his mother, where he was most contented. While there is some symbolic value in passing a child around to emphasize the responsibility of the larger community, it is best for the child's sake that he stay where he is happiest. Too many dedications are turned into an anxiety endurance contest by a scared, screaming baby. So, consider the children. The service is about children—about paying attention to a child.

The gesture of inviting the neighbors in acknowledges the likelihood that they will be more influential in the life of a child than blood family who live far away and are rarely seen. Neighbors' lives are often stronger models for a child's behavior than family or friends. Neighbors are teachers, for good or ill. To reach out to them is not only a recognition of the reality of the child's world, it is also a gift to them. You want them to know your values and the inside of the house where your child lives.

Good neighbors are made, not imagined or hoped for.

Finally, for emphasis, I say that the ceremony for Max is not a model in form for all welcomings of all babies. But it is a model for an attitude: to make the welcome out of who you are and what you are about. I insist that most of us have competent, sensitive, and thoughtful members of our circle of friends and family who can take the role of celebrant. There are many ministers among us—most of them do not work for a church. They are ordained—set aside as special—by the quality of their humanity and their special relationship with us.

❧

When it was learned that Max was born with a heart defect, the parents were devastated. They considered not having a ceremony, or waiting until after the surgery to make sure Max was going to make it. But having the ceremony was even more important now. Life is always at risk. We are all born into a graveyard. The tiny hole in Max's heart only intensified the place he held in his parents' hearts, and only magnified the reality of the need they had for support.

It never makes sense to wait until your life is in a perfect state of grace to celebrate its joys and passages. Never hesitate to celebrate.

(P.S. Max made it—you'd never know what he went through if you saw him chasing cats around the neighborhood these days.)

After a child is born, life goes on.

When a child is born, the drama lasts a couple of days, carried by its own energy. It's a timeless time—you are absorbed in the astonishing power of birth and the idea of parenthood. You are supported and cared for by those who helped you—family, friends, doctors, nurses, even strangers.

There is a moment, often recorded on film, of parents and child at the hospital threshold—mother, father, babe, and nurse. A liminal moment. After that picture, you're on your own.

"I never will forget that first night at home with my first child."

Ask just about any parent to carry on beyond that sentence, and you'll get a long and familiar tale. And you can enroll in all the advanced courses you want, and read all the recommended books, and get all the advice you can absorb, but nothing will or *can* completely prepare you for that sense of awed responsibility when it's clear *this child is in your hands*—totally dependent on you and your competence, such as it may be at the time.

It's probably one of the most intense twenty-four

hours of your life. Even if you get an easy baby, you still won't sleep much, because your emergency system is on full alert. On top of that, the baby needs food. Often. And if the baby is a blue screamer, well—after that first all-nighter, walking the floor, helpless in the face of both the child's distress and yours, you will be about five years older by dawn and have endured a rite of passage you had not anticipated. If you weren't an adult a week ago, you will have become one by morning. This is why they say children make babies, and then babies make adults. This is a rite of passage.

Remember the mess, the equipment, the smells, the unbelievable shambles this six pounds of humanity makes of the routines of your life? You have to regroup your resources and get organized. Remember getting organized?

Merging the needs of the child with your own needs leads to routine.

Routine that enables essential human functions is the rootstock of ritual—lifelong—especially if you look at what you're doing from the child's point of view. Sacred habits are being established.

Sleeping and waking, eating and bathing, getting dressed and undressed, talking and singing, holding and hugging, and, of course, eliminating body waste. For a period of about two and a half years, a child gets a diaper changed an average of six times a day. Around 5,400 times a child is laid on its back looking up at the face of a parent figure, is undressed, cleaned, powdered, talked to, touched and tickled, redressed, and given some form of physical affection—hugged, kissed, rocked, or played with. From the child's point of view, this rhythmic existence is all there is to life. It's more than taking care of business, it is ritual—that which gives structure and meaning to the child's life. This is how the world goes round.

If ritual for the child becomes hassle for the parents, some basic discontinuity occurs. That which gives the child pleasure and comfort and sustenance is confused with the parents' message that the same activities are a burden, a nuisance—something to get over quickly; then the land mines between parent and child get laid down early on and become buried in the sand of the family's past, to be stepped on sooner or later.

I know of few more fundamental secrets of child-rearing than this—that the parent understand that what may be routine chores for him or her are in fact all there is to the early life of the child. Respect for the ritual needs of the child leads to respect for the ritual patterns of the adult.

જ

As a child grows on, there is the matter of the child's child.

As a grandfather, I see the importance of this ritual behavior in ways I was too busy to think about as a parent. Three grandchildren keep me thinking.

There is the matter of reading the same story over and over, without any changes whatsoever. God forbid I should skip a page or a word. Heresy.

Their going-to-bed routine must be kept in its exact order—just like at home. Undressing, bath, jammies, teethbrush, story, tuck-in, goodnight.

Eating food at the same time in the same way. Despite the fact that I often eat dessert first at my house, this is not the way it's supposed to be, according to higher authorities, their parents. And after the children express initial amusement at my habits, they eat their vegetables first. They know where power resides. I have even been reported to their parents for my bad habits. Still, I really don't think the world will come to an end if you put chocolate sauce on vegetables.

Dressing in certain clothes in a certain way is likewise important. First underpants, then undershirt, then socks, then pants, then shirt, and finally shoes.

Knowing the rules and repeating them consistently counts. Don'ts and do's are expected and repeated in phrases I heard from my parents and passed on to my children.

Even the repetition of words and phrases is ritualized early on. Just recently, I was awakened long after bedtime by my four-year-old grandson, who was having trouble getting to sleep. "What's wrong?" "You didn't say sleep tight, don't let the bedbugs bite." "Sorry about that." We ambled back downstairs to his bed, said the ritual phrase, and he was sound asleep in no time.

When I crawled back into bed, my wife scratched my back a little, and I held her hand as we drifted off to dreamland. That's our "sleep tight" gesture. When she doesn't scratch or I don't reach for her hand, I know something's wrong, either with her or me or us.

This is not really kid stuff. It's a people thing.

I see it all in my own life. Daily.

In all the little ways, the rituals are there.

From beginning to end, the rituals of our lives sustain us.

The sacred habits of a lifetime.

Dead

Death is a black camel that lies down at every door.
Sooner or later you must ride the camel.

ARAB PROVERB

Children and adults do not look at death in the same way.

It is a mistake to assume that they do.

All you need do is watch a group of kindergarten kids at play, and you will witness much death activity—kids feigning death or getting "killed" and buried and dug up time and again, in what seems like a most casual fashion.

Children deal with death in a matter-of-fact way, and they live in a world of fantasy and imagination wherein death is reversible—characters are always dying and coming back to life again.

The way children come to have a more realistic view of death depends on how well parents have settled their own feelings about death and how parents handle life as well as death events.

The death of a pet is usually the first opportunity for teaching.

Let me tell you about the life and death of Snowball, a legend in her own time and place. Famous, but to a very small group of people. Worth knowing, if not well known.

You must know that guinea pigs are not from

Guinea and are not pigs. They are rodents from South America. Rodents, like rats and mice. A domesticated form of the cavy *(Cavia porcellus)*. Six to ten inches long, one to two pounds, come in many varieties—long hair, short hair, solid colors, and stripes. Major players in the pet industry.

Snowball was one of these rodents. White, with pink feet, eyes, and nose. She entered the life of the Thompson family under false pretenses, however. Four-year-old Lucy wanted a pet—a dog, please. Forty-year-old father did not want a dog, please. No room for a dog—small house, not much of a yard, and not much room in busy lives for a dog. Father knew who ended up taking care of dogs.

But the pet pressure was intense and insistent, and so just before Christmas one year, in a moment of sentimental weakness, Father visited a pet store during his lunch hour. He looked at the full range of rodents with a realistic eye, considering what he wanted loose in the house—he knew it would get loose—and how easy it would be to find. Guinea pigs at least had a size advantage. Also, he didn't want a pet that was smarter or faster than he was. So when the salesman told him guinea pigs had all the brains bred out of them and were really slow and stupid and didn't live long, the choice was clear. One guinea pig, coming up.

There were a couple of multicolored litters. Since it was snowing that day and the guinea pig was to be a Christmas present, the choice was obvious. He got the long-haired white one, a virgin female, too young to have been bred—about the size of a balled-up pair of gym socks. And about as animated. Perfecto.

Also he got all the equipment: cage, water dish, food dish, instruction manual, and food pellets. He declined the collar and leash. He wasn't going to walk a guinea pig.

Father decided not to try hiding the creature until Christmas Eve. It squeaked too loud to hide. He just lugged the cage into the kitchen when he got home and put it on the table. Taking the tiny, furry creature in his hands, he placed it on the table in front of his daughter and said, "Merry Christmas."

"What is it?" The child was fascinated.

"You mean you don't know?"

"No."

"Well, well . . . in that case . . . in *that* case . . . it really is something amazing . . . a kind of very small dog . . . from South America."

The mother gave the father her *you'll-be-sorry* look, but it was too late.

"A dog—really—oh, I really wanted a dog. What's its name?"

"I don't know—you have to name it—but it is snowing and she is white. She's a girl dog, so maybe we could name her Snow White?"

"Let's name her Snowball."

And that's how Snowball, the world's smallest dog, came to live with the Thompsons.

Snowball remained a dog for some time, actually, since the rest of the family and their friends went along with the ridiculous notion. Lucy and her father tried teaching Snowball dog tricks, and since Snowball had the personality of Silly Putty and would stay in almost any position she was placed in, there were times when you would swear she was playing dead, shaking hands, and rolling over—on retroactive command, of course.

It may have been true that Snowball was stupid, or maybe eccentric, or maybe just friendly. It was hard to tell. It was also hard not to appreciate that, for whatever reason, Snowball was a *great* guinea pig.

By the time some neighborhood kid spilled the beans and told Lucy the truth about her ''dog,'' it didn't matter anymore. Lucy and Snowball had bonded, life to life. Even Lucy enjoyed the game of confusing strangers by introducing them to her ''dog.'' Lucy had her father's sense of humor.

Snowball let Lucy dress her up in doll clothes, and often appeared at mealtimes in a hat and dress. Snowball and Lucy became inseparable—where Lucy was, Snowball was. The family learned in time that the sound of Snowball's contented squeaking from Lucy's room at bedtime meant all was well in the house, especially with Lucy.

Snowball grew roly-poly fat, and her white fur comically grew in many directions so that, in her dress and hat, she resembled nothing more than a tiny little old lady who had just got out of bed and hadn't bothered to comb her hair. Only the sourest personality did not look at Snowball and laugh. Snowball was the house comic act. Lucy spoke for her, using Snowball as a ventriloquist's dummy. It was hard to be depressed or unhappy with Lucy and Snowball onstage.

–

When Snowball grew up, she had regular menstrual periods. Lucy's father took the opportunity to talk with Lucy about how guinea pigs are made. They talked about family planning, too, since one guinea pig was really quite enough responsibility for Lucy. Maybe Snowball would get pregnant someday, but not now.

In her fourth year, Snowball began losing her fur. In no time at all, she was hairless—just a fat, warm pink lump. It was even harder not to look at Snowball and laugh. She was the talk of the neighborhood, and Lucy charged a five-cent admission to see "SNOWBALL, THE BALD WONDER DOG!"

A trip to the vet was an educational experience. Snowball was old for a guinea pig and was experiencing a major hormone imbalance. The vet suggested two courses of action: hormone and vitamin shots along with a hysterectomy—or else she could be put to sleep and replaced by a new pet. While a couple dozen new guinea pigs could be bought for the cost of Snowball's treatment, there was no real choice. Snowball was family. The whole family loved their dinky dog. They had not expected to have to get a hysterectomy for a guinea pig, but what had to be done was done. The mother said, "Maybe Lucy's teacher should be warned in advance about what's coming to show-and-tell next week."

—

Lucy nursed Snowball back to health with great devotion. The whole family rejoiced at her rejuvenation. But some months later there was blood in Snowball's cage. Snowball quit eating. She barely squeaked. The vet confirmed the worst. Cancer. Snowball's days were numbered. She would soon be in terrible pain and then die. "Die?" "Yes." "You mean forever?" "Yes." Lucy was heartbroken.

Snowball went home for a couple of days for good-byes. Dressed in her best hat and dress, she was the guest of honor at meals. Snowball stories were told, with the laughter and tears you might expect. Her birthday was celebrated early, and she got her Christmas presents, even though Christmas was still a long way off.

The heavy questions came up. The ones already discussed at bedtime for the last few days, but that got discussed again and again: "Where do guinea pigs go after they die?" "Does it hurt to die?" "When I die, will it be like Snowball?" "Does everything in the universe die?" "Why?" "Why?"

On Wednesday morning, the family stayed home from work and school. Snowball was driven to the vet and put to sleep painlessly. Placed in her favorite sleeping place—an old brown-leather house slipper, which was put in a small, lidded basket lined with straw and placed in the front seat between Lucy and her dad. The family car became a hearse for the ride home.

Snowball, the tiny wonder dog from South America, living under an assumed name and disguised as a guinea pig, was laid to rest in a grave dug underneath the willow tree in the backyard. Lucy and her mom and dad thanked Snowball for all the good times and filled in the grave. And marked it with a large flat stone on which Lucy had written in paint: "Happy Days, Snowball."

⟡

This story, of course, is not about pets.

It's about any life and death. It's about the deep attachments we make to other living things. It's about the obligatory rituals of hello and good-bye when we become attached to the life around us. And it's about how we help children understand the basic lessons of existence.

To an outsider, Snowball is just a guinea pig.

But Snowball was also a teacher from whom Lucy learned about responsibility, affection, reproduction, imagination, sorrow, and death. Lucy's grandmother is dying now, and Snowball made dealing with that easier for everyone in the family. Snowball, Grandma, Mother, Father, and someday Lucy. It is the way of living things. All of them. Now Lucy knows.

CERTIFICATE OF DEATH

USE BLACK INK ONLY

STATE FILE NUMBER

LOCAL REGISTRATION DISTRICT AND CERTIFICATE NUMBER

DECEDENT PERSONAL DATA

1A. NAME OF DECEDENT—First (Given)

1B. Middle

1C. Last (Family)

2A. DATE OF DEATH—Mo., Day, Yr.

2B. Hour

3. Sex

4. Race

5. Hispanic—Specify
☐ Yes   ☐ No

6. Date of Birth—Mo. Day. Yr.

7. Age in Years | If Under 1 Year: Months / Days | If Under 24 Hours: Hours / Minutes

8. State of Birth

9. Citizen of What Country

10A. Full Name of Father

10B. State of Birth

11A. Full Maiden Name of Mother

11B. State of Birth

12. Military Service
19 ____ TO 19 ____   ☐ None

13. Social Security No.

14. Marital Status

15. Name of Surviving Spouse (If Wife Enter Maiden Name)

16A. Usual Occupation

16B. Usual Kind of Business or Industry

16C. Usual Employer

16D. Years in Occupation

17. Education — Years Completed

USUAL RESIDENCE

18A. Residence—Street and Number or Location

18B. City

18C. Zip Code

18D. County

18E. Number of Years in the County

18F. State or Foreign Country

PLACE OF DEATH

19A. Place of Death

19B. If Hospital Specify One: IP, ERR/OP, DOA

19C. County

19D. Street Address—Street and Number or Location

19E. City

20. Name, Relationship, Mailing Address and Zip Code of Informant

CAUSE OF DEATH

21. DEATH WAS CAUSED BY: (Enter Only One Cause Per Line for A, B, and C)

TIME INTERVAL BETWEEN ONSET AND DEATH

IMMEDIATE CAUSE (A) ▲

DUE TO (B) ▲

DUE TO (C) ▲

25. Other Significant Conditions Contributing to Death But Not Related to Cause Given in 21

22. Was Death Reported to Coroner Referral Number
☐ Yes   ☐ No

23. Was Biopsy Performed?
☐ Yes   ☐ No

24A. Was Autopsy Performed?
☐ Yes   ☐ No

24B. Was It Used in Determining Cause of Death?
☐ Yes   ☐ No

26. Was Operation Performed for Any Condition in Item 21 or 25? If Yes, List Type of Operation and Date

PHYSICIAN'S CERTIFICATION

I Certify That to the Best of My Knowledge Death Occurred at the Hour, Date and Place Stated From the Causes Stated.

27A. Decedent Attended Since Month, Day, Year

Decedent Last Seen Alive Month, Day, Year

27B. Signature and Degree or Title of Certifier ▲

27C. Certifyer's License Number

27D. Date Signed

27E. Type Attending Physician's Name and Address

EUPHEMISMS

Died	Liquidated
Resting in peace	Left this world
Curtains	Croaked
Perished	Breathed her last
Cashed in his chips	Met his Maker
Bought the farm	Laid to rest
No longer with us	Bit the dust
Passed on	In the great beyond
Snuffed	Asleep in the deep
Gave up the ghost	Departed
Kicked the bucket	His time was up
Gone home	Out of her misery
Went to her eternal reward	Ended it all
Gone to heaven	Dead as a doorknob
Succumbed	Dead 'n' gone

While visiting friends on the Greek island of Crete, I was caught up in a funeral. There is an ancient Orthodox monastery very near the small village of Kolimbari at the west end of the island. An old monk had died—a man much revered by the community. His body was washed but not embalmed. Then it was dressed in the simple daily garb of his vocation and laid out in a plain wooden coffin and placed in the chapel of the monastery. There, those who knew him came to pay their respects and say prayers for his soul.

On the day appointed, more than two hundred people of all ages gathered for the formal service, filling the chapel and spilling out into the courtyard. At the end of the service, as a single bell tolled, the coffin was shouldered by six strong men and carried slowly along a steep path to a graveyard on the hill, where the reverend father was buried. After a final service of chanting and prayer, the villagers went about their lives.

While I did not understand a word of the service, I was deeply moved by the spirit of the occasion. I felt both comfortable and comforted—rather than ill at ease, as I most often feel at funerals.

Funerals have been conducted this way in this village for a time beyond memory. The religious customs of the Greek Orthodox Church so permeate the lives of people that when someone dies, everyone knows what is to be done and how to participate in it. Life and death are so carefully interwoven that the rites of passage from one to another are seamless and unquestioned.

It is a mistake to apply a tourist's point of view here. This was not a quaint and charming event in the lives of peasants still living in the past. It took place within a community of modern Greeks. In myriad ways, they look and act and think and dress like contemporary Europeans and Americans. Many speak English and German. They drive Japanese and German cars, see the wider world through television, and have every modern household convenience and agricultural advancement at their service.

Yet, there are important differences. It is a homogeneous community. They are all Greeks. Most of them live out their lives in or near the village where they were born. From birth to death, the events of their daily lives are intertwined. They see each other be born, grow up, live, and die. Their culture and their church are likewise bound up together. They live and die in the embrace of the Greek Orthodox Church.

Which means that when someone dies, every person knows what is to be done and knows his or her part in the rituals of death and mourning. It is done as it has always been for as long as anyone remembers. Even now, even in the larger towns, this is the case.

In contrast, consider a death in a modern American city. Many of those at a funeral do not know one another well, if at all, and do not share common religious or cultural traditions regarding rites of passage. There are exceptions, of course: within the ethnic immigrant enclaves in major cities, the Orthodox Jewish community, and the Mormon towns of Utah, among others.

In the past, when our country was still largely rural, our practices were similar in every way to what is done in Greece. But those days are gone. We are a sophisticated, multifaceted urban society now.

Death, in our time, has been given over to institutions.

Eighty percent of us die in a hospital. If we die elsewhere, 911 is called, and the police, fire department, ambulance company, emergency room, funeral home, lawyers, courts, insurance companies, accountants, churches and ministers, cemeteries, and several government agencies become involved. All have their rules and protocols. For most of us, once we die, we are no longer in the care of our families and friends—strangers and institutions take over. Though we may witness the portrayal of thousands of deaths in movies and on television, it is rare for any of us to see a dead person, much less touch or care for the deceased.

Death is not in our school curriculum.

Except perhaps in a biology course, death and dying are not considered.

Instead of a normal part of life, death is treated as an unexpected emergency, something that happens when the medical community fails. We always die "of something"—as though if it weren't for that disease or accident, we could have lived on. "Old age" or "worn out" or "life completed" are concepts not found on death certificates or in obituaries.

Death in our time means crisis.

When someone dies and I'm called upon as a minister, I'm struck by the tone of "something awful has happened." And the response to the crisis is haste. As soon as possible, things must be done: The living must put aside their lives to meet the emergency of death—arrangements must be made, people must be called, decisions must be reached—all as soon as possible. Urgency dominates. Because they were not expecting this to happen. "She died unexpectedly." That's what we say.

So many times I have met with families who had no clue as to what to do or where to begin. They don't know the wishes of the deceased, much less if there is a will and where it might be. The possibility of death has never been addressed in that family. Instead of the last rites, we deal with the last crisis. It's no wonder funerals often seem awkward and painful. We are not prepared.

It doesn't have to be this way.

I will go further and say it should not be this way.

As I invited you to a wedding and the celebration of the birth of a child, let me take you with me to a funeral. A really fine funeral that celebrates a wonderful life and illustrates how much life is gained by preparing well for being dead.

&

For now you only need know that the deceased is an eighty-year-old retired schoolteacher named Martha Carter, and she planned her own ceremony, which takes the form of a committal at graveside.

It's a lovely, quiet old cemetery on a hillside. Well kept, lots of trees—the first flowers of spring are in bloom. It's April. A dark green awning has been erected over the grave, and there are brown metal folding chairs on three sides for close family and friends.

Interestingly enough, nobody is wearing black—not even the minister or funeral directors. All of the women and most of the men present are dressed for spring—in bright colors or flowered prints. This apparent dress code alone tells you much about the deceased and her ideas about what a funeral should be like. She wanted it this way. Her agenda was and is Life.

–

Another unexpected touch is the traditional jazz band that comes walking up the cemetery drive—trumpet, slide trombone, tuba, clarinet, and snare drum. They're playing a slow, dignified tune that still has the fine edge of swing in it. It's hard not to smile when they make their entrance. The band finishes playing while standing a little way off from the gravesite and ends the tune with an "amen" chord. The minister stands up, facing us across the grave, opens a Bible, and begins.

For everything there is a season,
And a time and purpose for every matter under
heaven.
A time to be born, and a time to die;
A time to weep, and a time to laugh;
A time to mourn, and a time to dance;
A time to keep silence, and a time to speak;
For everything there is a season,
And a time and purpose for every matter under
heaven.

We have come together on this fine day in spring-time to celebrate the life of Martha Lee Olson McBride Carter, and on behalf of Martha and her family, I welcome you to this service. Here we shall honor her memory and respect her wishes.

We have come to mourn and to remember a friend and companion.

We have come to affirm life itself and our part in it.

We have come to consider death and how we shall meet it.

This is a unique occasion in that Martha Carter spent part of the last year of her life carefully planning the affairs of her death and thinking through what she wanted to happen at her funeral. In all the years I have been a minister, I have never met any-one who more clearly understood that death is a part of life or who more carefully crafted a rite of passage reflecting that wisdom.

Martha included her family in her planning be-cause she wanted, as a parent, both to meet their needs and to be as instructive about death as she had been about life. She told me she didn't think her kids always paid much attention to what she said, but they always watched what she did. When it came to dying, she meant to show them how it might be done well.

She left it to her family and friends to say what they felt should be said, but she asked that they not go on too long—she thought most funerals were too wordy.

With that admonition, I call upon her oldest grandson, Harlan Adams.

—

A very tall and skinny young man in his early twenties stands awkwardly by the grave, looks down for a moment, takes a manuscript from his coat pocket, speaks:

My family asked me to give a factual summary of my grandmother's life so that those who didn't know her well might better understand some of the memo-ries others will share.

Martha Lee Olson was born in Chicago, Illinois, on January 20, 1914.

ltn

And she died here in Seattle on April first of this year, at age eighty.

It would have pleased her to know she died on April Fool's Day.

The only daughter of Danish immigrants—her father, John, worked for the railroad in many capacities during his life, and his wife, Ingrid, ran the household, raised her child, and managed a huge garden that fed the family all through the Great Depression.

Though the family moved from railroad town to railroad town as she was growing up, they were living in Chicago again when Martha graduated from high school. Martha went off to the University of Illinois to become a teacher. Both she and her mother worked at various part-time jobs to make college possible.

While she was in college, her father was transferred to Seattle by the railroad, but Martha finished at Illinois before coming out to join her parents and taking a job teaching sixth grade at Franklin Elementary School.

When the Second World War broke out, she began working as a volunteer at the USO to help the morale of the thousands of young soldiers passing through Seattle on the way to serve in the Pacific. It was there that she met Marine Sergeant Fred McBride, and married him a week before he shipped out.

Nine months later, she gave birth to her first child, Fred McBride, Jr.

She never saw her husband again—he was killed in combat in 1943.

Her father was killed in a railroad accident in 1944.

To add to the tragedy, twenty-five years later, Lieutenant Fred McBride, Jr., was also killed in combat, in 1968, in Vietnam.

After the war, Grandmother started work on her master's degree at the University of Washington. While there she met fellow student, and my grandfather, Edward Carter, a G.I. just home from the war in Europe. They were married in 1947.

My mom, Hannah, was born the next year, and her brother Alan a year later.

Grandmother Martha's own mother lived with her until 1955, when she passed away after a long struggle with cancer.

When Martha's children started school, she began teaching again, at the Seaside High School, where she taught English literature until she retired in 1979.

She was widowed again, in 1964, when my grandfather died of heart failure.

For the last thirty years of her life, she lived alone, investing herself in the lives of her children, grandchildren, and former students.

When she retired, she pursued her dreams of traveling around the United States and Europe. When *her health and age brought her traveling days to an end, she became involved in all kinds of volunteer work—with the American Red Cross, the League of Women Voters, the Council of Churches, and the Traditional Jazz Society.*

When I asked her once what church she belonged to, she said she belonged to them all—mostly because of her work with the Council of Churches. I know she was raised Lutheran, married an Irish Catholic the first time and an inactive Baptist the second time. When I was asked to drive Grandmother to church, I never knew where we were going to go. Sometimes it was to the Greek Orthodox early mass, sometimes to the Episcopal vespers service, and sometimes to the Quaker morning meeting. She found meaning and friends wherever she worshiped.

She lived the last two years of her life depending on a dialysis machine for kidney function, but she never complained. To her it was an opportunity to put her affairs in order. When she was too weak to get out of bed, she made the decision to stop treatment and to die, which she did a week later.

I've given you the basic facts of the life of a remarkable woman. I could talk about what she meant to me and tell stories about her for hours. I really loved and respected her. However, if she was here, Grandma would say I have done what I was asked to do and said more than enough and should sit down.

So I will.

—

The minister stands and says:

Martha Carter knew a lot about pain and sorrow.

Martha Carter was close to death all her life.

All four of her grandparents died during her childhood.

Her first husband and first son were killed in wartime.

In the middle years of her life, both of her parents and her second husband died. And, as she explained to me, half of her friends and acquaintances had died during the last ten years. She said she was tired of death and tired of dreary funerals, and especially hated having to show up for this one today. She wished there could be some laughter at her own funeral. When I asked her how to do this, she suggested I share a story she heard George Burns tell.

A teacher was asking her students what their fathers did. All the pupils named their fathers' occupations—plumber, clerk, fireman, etc. One boy didn't volunteer, so the teacher asked, "Well, Billy, what does your father do?" And Billy replied that his father didn't do anything—he was dead. "Well," asked the teacher, "what did he do before he died?" And Billy answered: "He went AAAAGggggghhhhh."

If you asked Martha Carter what she did, she said "teacher"—even after she retired, she never said "retired teacher"—she was always a teacher. Her family has asked one of her former pupils, Dr. Richard Havens, to speak about her teaching.

—

Dr. Havens is a middle-aged scholar, bearded, dressed to blend into his habitat—conservative tweed suit with vest—but oddly enough, wearing a boldly striped black-and-white shirt and sporting a pink-and-yellow silk tie. As he stands to speak, he pulls the flamboyant tie out of his vest and looks down at it. In his other hand, he is holding a large shopping bag. He says:

Mrs. Carter gave me this tie. And I say "Mrs. Carter" because no matter how old you get, you always address your teachers as you did in high school, and you always feel a little like that kid you used to be when you are around them. You can't ever be peers. I can't imagine ever calling her "Martha." I can't believe she's dead—because if she can die, then so can I.

Anyhow. About the tie. She ran into me four years ago in a bookstore. After the usual greetings, she stood back to look at me and take stock. I was wearing this suit. As she noticed and you can see, I have adopted the disguise of college professor. She was appalled. She said I looked so old and stuffy and serious. She gave me a hard time. How could I stand up in front of young people and teach them anything exciting if I looked like a cadaver? She said I was going to look dead for a long time before I actually was put in a coffin. She said I just had to lighten up. She remembered that I was a good dancer in high school, but she bet I hadn't been dancing in years. And she was right.

So she took me by the hand and off we went to a men's store up the street where she announced to the clerk that this young man, meaning me, needs help. Insisting I take off my coat and vest and remove the drab tie I was wearing, she looked over the selection of ties and picked this one. While I was dutifully knotting it around my neck, she took the clerk's scissors and cut my old tie in half and dropped it in the wastebasket.

She had the clerk put my vest in a bag to carry with me, and then, helping me into my coat, she had me stand in front of the mirror and said I looked much better and that I should loosen up and I would live longer. She said getting old too soon wasn't good for me. She paid for the tie and was out the door before I could thank her.

When I was in school, I thought she taught English literature and writing.

On reflection, I know that what she really taught was how to learn and how to live. I went into teaching because of her. The gift of the tie reminded me that I had paid too much attention to English literature and not enough to life.

Pausing, Dr. Havens removes his tweed jacket and vest and, laying them aside, he pulls a lime-green linen jacket out of the shopping bag and puts it on. Out of the pocket of the jacket, he takes a red foam-rubber clown nose and sticks it onto his nose. He looks so wonderfully, foolishly transformed that we cannot help but laugh and applaud.

I don't dress this way all the time, you know. I bought this jacket to wear for this service. I think Mrs. Carter would approve. I find it's hard work getting young again after you've decided to be old.

If you ask anyone about the influences in their lives, most people will start by saying, "Well, there was this teacher." And the teachers they talk about always seem to have the same qualities. They were hard—had high standards and demanded the best not only of their students but of themselves. They respected their students and demanded respect in return. They were good at teaching because they loved learning themselves. And they taught both by what they did in class and by how they lived outside the class. Great teachers are more like great coaches—they see themselves on the sidelines doing everything they can do to make the players do as well as they can in the game, knowing that losses and failure are not shameful but often more instructive than winning.

She had this wonderful way of beginning a course. She gave each student a piece of paper with his name on it and a grade—an "A." She wanted us to know she started out thinking the best of us, and it was left to us to change her view.

Mrs. Carter was a great teacher.

Three specific examples, among many, stand out in my mind.

She began preparing for her retirement about five years before she was sixty-five. She wanted to travel in France and decided to learn French. Instead of going off to some cram class in the evening, she enrolled herself in the freshman French class in our high school and insisted to her colleague that she wanted to be treated just like any other student and held to the same standards. Imagine! A teacher wanting to learn something! Not in secret, but right there in front of us!

She also wanted to know what it felt like to be a student in our school. And though she worked very hard, she wasn't very good at French. And we knew it. Because when the first report cards came out, everybody wanted to know her grade, and she showed us when we asked: a "C." We were astonished. But she said everybody wasn't good at the same thing, and she would just have to work harder.

That she had experienced defeat meant she knew what the rest of us experienced sometimes. She could have quit. We thought she was humiliated, but she said ignorance was a sign of hope, not failure. And she took French for three years. She got successful senior French students to tutor her, and she ate lunch at a table in the cafeteria where only French could be spoken. She subscribed to French magazines and newspapers and struggled through them. Every one of her English students who took French became her French teacher. When she moved up to "B"'s her second year, we all rejoiced with her. And when she made "A"'s the last year, we insisted that she be placed on the school honor roll and made a special member of the Honor Society.

Mrs. Carter had learned French. But more than that, she taught the whole school something none of us will ever forget: Hope and tenacity and hard work can pay off—you can *do better. She taught the students how to learn. She taught her colleagues how to teach.*

The second memory of Mrs. Carter I want to mention is kin to the first. Her interest in the lives of her students was legendary. Not in a personal, snooping sense, but in an educational way. If she knew you knew something she didn't know much about, she would inquire of you. A football linebacker would find himself explaining how he learned plays or how he knew what to do when the other team had the ball. The guys who were interested in cars would find themselves under the hood with Mrs. Carter, explaining how a carburetor worked. A kid who played guitar in a band would get grilled on the difference between a reggae beat and a rock-and-roll beat. If a student was doing well in her class but didn't seem to be going about writing papers the way Mrs. Carter suggested, she wanted to know how the student actually went about the task; and if Mrs. Carter learned something she could pass on, she wouldn't claim it as her idea, but she would explain in class that So-and-so did it another way and ask So-and-so to explain it. We called her "the Chief Investigator" and

"Inspector Carter" behind her back. What I know now is that she was interested in how minds work—she respected ours, especially if they worked differently from her own.

But the last memory is the one being made here now. I knew she had complete kidney failure and didn't have long to live. I'm deeply moved by the care she put into preparing for her own death when she knew her time had come; the insistence that this occasion be about life; the request that we not come in black or be too solemn; the jazz band and the party tomorrow night; and the little odds and ends she sent all of us the past year. What an exit. What a classy way to go.

When I was young, she taught me how to think, how to learn; later, she taught me how to loosen up. And being here now I realize she still isn't through with me. She's taught me how to die.

—

The minister stands and remains silent for a time. Then he speaks:

Jennifer Jason was Martha Carter's student in high school. Eight years later she became Martha's daughter-in-law when she married Martha's son, Alan, and subsequently became the mother of Martha's first grandchild. She has been asked to speak on behalf of the family.

—

One look at Jennifer Jason Carter and you surmise that she must be very much like her mother-in-law at the same age—short chestnut hair, rosy complexion, trimly dressed in a yellow suit, she gives an impression of confidence, intelligence, and vitality. She says:

Our family talked with Martha about this service for most of an afternoon just before she died. That evening, after Martha had fallen asleep, we talked for hours. That was part of Martha's memorial service—as all the memories of her came back to her family. We laughed and cried and sat sometimes in silence.

It was clear to Hannah and Alan that they could not begin to eulogize their mother here today—they wouldn't know where to stop and wouldn't be able to finish because of the strength of their feelings. I'm pleased to speak for them.

We asked Dick Havens to speak first because Martha was above all else a teacher—both at school and with her family. The best moments of her life came when those two worlds overlapped. In her prime, she seemed so strong, so serious, and so sure of herself that her students thought of her as invulnerable. And, even on her worst days, she managed to teach.

I remember one day in class when she surprised us by being irritable and ill-tempered. She got angry at one student and then dismissed the class early because she felt none of us had really done our homework. "Out, out," she snapped, pointing at the door. Stunned and cowed, we silently collected our belongings and passed into the hallway. Before we got very far, she came to the door, and in a voice so soft we hardly heard her, she called after us to please come back. She was in tears. When we had resumed our seats, she sat down behind her desk and, with tears streaming down her cheeks, told us she was ashamed of herself and how sorry she was for the way she had acted. It wasn't our fault. She said she was not feeling well, had not been sleeping well, and had some difficult things to deal with in her personal life. But she apologized for taking her feelings out on us, and since she knew we had bad days sometimes, too, she felt we would understand. Half the class ended up hugging her and comforting her.

It was the first time in my entire life an adult had apologized to me for anything. And if Martha Carter could make a mistake and apologize, then so could I. I don't remember a lot of things about English literature, but I will never forget that moment of being taught the power of integrity. Because of her I have always apologized to her son and her grandchildren when I lost my temper.

Speaking of temper, Martha Carter had one—the kind that could remove paint and a layer of hide. She was not without her flaws. Her energy and ability could be overwhelming at times. Sometimes I avoided her because she always seemed so organized. She didn't have much patience with sloppy thinking. If you got into an intellectual discussion with her, you'd better have your facts right and your homework done, or she'd eat you alive and you'd feel so dumb you wanted to hide under a chair. Her virtue was a little hard to take, too—she didn't lie and she didn't cheat, and she was tough on those who did. She was so independent you wondered if she ever really needed anybody—there was so little she could not do for herself.

It took me years to understand that the reason she came on so strong is that she had to be strong all her life—she had no choice. She had so much death and sickness to deal with—she had to work and raise a family alone—and she knew there was nobody to fall back on. Her strength armored her weaknesses.

When she was dying, I was astonished when she told me she had been scared all her life. She wasn't afraid of anything anymore. Typically, she made a joke of this by saying that she had always wanted to have a quiet little place in the country all by herself and now she was going to get it.

If you want to know if she was a successful parent, all you have to do is look at the lives of Hannah and Alan and how they are with their own children, and the answer is yes. In a conversation between just the two of us, Martha said that of course she loved her children as any mother should, but when she stepped back and looked at them with her most critical eye, she also really liked them, admired them, and was proud of them.

I knew Martha Carter at several stages of my life and hers. What amazed me is the way she continued to change and grow until the day she died. When she retired from teaching, she said she was also retiring from being a respectable matron. She let her hair grow long, stopped wearing serious clothes, bought a pickup truck to drive, and moved to a tiny house with a huge yard so she could raise the garden of her dreams. She traveled, did volunteer work, and took ballroom dancing lessons.

For exercise, she took up walking. She didn't like sitting around making small talk, so if you wanted to visit with her, you had to go for a walk—and she could walk forever. On her walks, she was still the Chief Investigator—Inspector Carter—always looking into whatever interested her, talking with strangers, and marching right into people's yards to see flowers that attracted her attention.

As she grew older and her friends began to die, she said she needed younger friends and some new ideas. So she went back to the university to study art and art history and be with the younger generation.

About five years ago, when she was seventy-five years old, the family was a little surprised to get a call one Sunday night asking for one of us to pick her up at Norway Hall because she was unable to drive. We didn't know what on earth she was doing at a dance hall and couldn't imagine her too drunk to drive. She wasn't drunk—she had sprained her ankle while dancing. That's how we found out she had taken an interest in traditional New Orleans–style jazz. When bands she liked played at the Norway

Hall on Sunday nights, she went to listen and dance. She said it was a lot more comforting than church sometimes.

Martha Carter and I had a rich relationship. She was my mentor. And I loved her with all my heart. And I give my family fair warning: I plan to be as alive as she was for as long as I live. When I'm old and you wonder where I am on weekends, look for me at Norway Hall. And if anybody wonders why, I can say my mother-in-law drove me to it.

–

Jennifer moves to sit beside her husband and children, and there is quiet again—only the sound of a slight breeze moving the leaves of the trees.

The minister introduces Fred Ambler, the trombone player in the band.

He's a plump, balding, middle-aged man—a little ill at ease with speaking.

–

Well, I'm really glad I came today. I didn't know all these things about Martha. I just thought she was this neat old lady who showed up from time to time and helped out the Jazz Society by selling tickets at the door and putting up decorations. She was a pretty good dancer, too. When she called me a couple of weeks before she died and asked if the band would play at her funeral, I didn't quite know what to say. I know this is a New Orleans tradition, but our band had never done it, and we didn't know what to play. But she did. She picked out all the tunes—some because she liked the name of the song and some because she liked to dance to them.

When we came up the drive a little while ago, we played "Mama's Gone Goodbye"; in a minute we'll play "His Eye Is on the Sparrow"; and at the end, "When the Saints Go Marching In." During the reception, she asked us to play "Gimme a Break," "My Bucket's Got a Hole in It," "Making Whoopee," and "Muskrat Ramble," among others. Tomorrow night there's a party at Norway Hall— potluck supper at six and music and dancing until nine. Martha Carter paid for it, so it's free and you're invited. She asked me to say to you that if you don't know much about our music or how to dance to it, come anyway, maybe you'll learn something you can use. Thank you.

Fred Ambler walks over to where the rest of the band is standing in the shade of some trees, and the band plays, "His Eye Is on the Sparrow, and I Know He Watches Me"—in slow tempo, with solos all around.

—

After a pause, the minister stands alongside the grave once again, holding an envelope in one hand.

Martha Carter was not an official member of my church, though she attended on occasion and we were casually acquainted. It was a little surprising to get her call about a month ago asking me to conduct her funeral, saying something like "My time has come, Reverend, and you're my man.'' I was a little taken aback at first, but after helping her arrange this service, I feel as though I had won an important honor—the Martha Carter Funeral Award.

She insisted that the service be brief, an honest reflection of her life and beliefs, and above all, considerate of the needs and feelings of her family and friends. Her *wishes were not her first concern. She wanted to make sure that this service was as inclusive as possible and that there was time for people to have their own thoughts and not feel imposed upon.*

And, as you might expect, she wanted the last word.

The minister holds up the envelope for all to see.

On the outside, in her handwriting, it says, *A Note from Martha.*

He tears open the sealed envelope, takes out a folded note, and reads aloud:

–

All in all, I've had a wonderful life.
Thank you all for your part in it.
When death appeared at my door, I was
expecting him.
I put on my dancing shoes and went.
You do the same.
      Good-bye, with love—Martha.

–

The minister shows the note to all and says:
The legacy of Martha Carter is not the dry residue of death. She left behind the sweet taste of the fine

wine of life. When I think now of Martha Carter, a voice in my head says, "I hope I live and die as well as she has."

And another voice, perhaps Martha's, replies: "So?—what's keeping you?"

Will you please stand.

You are invited to join us under the trees for refreshments—the family would like to greet all of you. And, of course, you are invited to the dance tomorrow night. Finally, a request: At the end of the service, will you please stop by the grave, take a handful of dirt, and place it on Martha's urn. She wanted her family and friends to bury her.

And now, let us join in silent prayer, each in his own way.

—

(Silence.)

–

We are grateful for Martha Lee Olson McBride Carter.
For her example—of how to live and how to die.
Dust to dust, ashes to ashes, God bless her.
God bless us all.
Amen.

–

The minister picks up the small wooden box that has been sitting on a table at the end of the grave, places it in the concrete vault below, scatters a handful of dirt on it, and moves on as members of the family come to do the same. The band strikes up "The Saints" and marches off down the driveway, stepping lively, blowing strong.

For Martha Carter, ignorance was always an enemy.

When her first husband died, he left no will, and she knew nothing about his legal and financial affairs. Because he was killed in combat in wartime, she was at the mercy of the bureaucracies of both the federal and state governments. She had to engage an attorney, and even then it took almost two years to collect documents, file forms, get the estate probated, and finally settle all her husband's affairs.

It was an awful, awful experience—she lived with his death daily for two years in a most painful way. A part of her life was taken away because she was not free to make any decisions involving money or property until the estate was settled. It was bad enough being a young widow with a child—but to have to endure all the frustrations built into the legal machinery was more than she thought she could bear at times. Her parents, though alive and well at the time, were little help—they were too fearful of death themselves and couldn't talk about it with her. If only her husband had left a simple will. . . .

Martha said she was like everybody else in that she didn't learn her lesson the first time. Or the second time. And beyond. She went through a similar experience when her father, son, and second husband died. Everybody puts off planning for death, which means that others suffer the consequences of our inaction.

My knowledge backs Martha's—about seventy percent of those who die, die intestate—without a will or any adequate instructions for their executors or next of kin. And in doing so, leave confusion and pain and frustration as major bequests to their families.

As Martha pointed out, the problem is that we are reluctant to talk about death. We're afraid, for one thing, and ignorant for another. But since we think death is always a long way off, we think we can deal with it when the time comes.

Martha was determined to settle her affairs well— not just think about it.

Though her affairs were not complicated, and though she had a basic will drawn up when her second husband died, she wanted to make sure her affairs really were in order. Times change—laws change. The year dialysis began, she consulted her attorney, read a current book about estate planning, and made the necessary adjustments to her will so that the costs and complications of estate probate were avoided.

At the same time, she made what she felt was an equally important step. She began a series of conversations with her family. She said, ''As hard as it may be to talk about death matters, if you hide anything from your family now, they will be sorry later. I know.''

First she discussed her legal and financial affairs with them and did what was possible to transfer her property and power of attorney to her children, especially to her daughter, who the family agreed was to be the formal executor of her estate.

At about the same time, she made sure that her family had access to her safe-deposit box at the bank and knew just where her legal and financial records were kept. Her daughter went along with her to meet with her attorney when the final will was notarized.

Next she started writing a Letter of Instruction.

This began as a written description of her wishes about her funeral and continued with thoughts about the disposition of personal possessions not involved in the settlement of her estate—gifts to family and friends. Since this was not a binding legal document, it soon became a sentimental journal of her last year of life.

Martha realized that she had more than *things* to leave behind—there were thoughts and feelings to leave as well. She started writing personal notes to be mailed after she died—some to be mailed as much as a year later. A few of the small gifts were not to be made until some time had passed.

In years past, when members of her family died, she found that society treated the funeral as the end of the matter. Yet her own mourning went on for such a long time afterward. She knew her friends had to get on with their lives, and she didn't want to impose her ongoing sorrow on them. But she needed sympathy and kindness at times when she couldn't ask. It frustrated her that nobody else seemed to know or care. She recalled once taking out her anguish on one of her classes—it was the anniversary of her son's death.

Several of her friends had lost husbands in recent years, and it was her custom to write short letters of consolation at the time of death and then write much longer letters after six months or a year had passed. She knew from her own experience it was at these later times that empathy was most needed—that gestures of caring were most appreciated. It was on these anniversary dates that she sent flowers—it was the living who needed them later on, not the dead at the funeral.

So it was that a year after her own death, her children and closest friends received notes and flowers *from her.* This really happened—because Martha had entrusted the task to me. And in doing so, taught me how to minister to those who grieve.

Notice that I keep emphasizing teaching. *All* of us are teachers. All of us fill that role of educator in the lives of children and friends, even strangers. Somebody looks up to each one of us to set an example. We know this because we look to others for inspiration. We learn from what they do and are. Teach well.

Having arranged her legal, financial, and emotional affairs as far as words and numbers on paper
could go, Martha turned to her funeral arrangements.
Since she had made arrangements for others, she
knew just how much the costs could be. If she did
nothing and her family turned the matter over to a
funeral home, she figured it would cost as much as
five thousand dollars. She liked the candor of one funeral director who told her she could spend all she
wanted on embalming and a casket, but the same
thing would happen to her sooner or later—dust and
bones. In one year without embalming and maybe
fifteen or twenty years with embalming. What difference did it make? Dust and bones, no matter what.
And the whole earth would fall into the sun someday,
and everything would be cremated then, he said, so
why wait?

She liked this guy—he dealt a straight hand.

The same candid man also told her if she was cremated, she shouldn't have her ashes spread in gar-
dens or under plants—especially roses; too much
calcium would kill them—he also had learned the
hard way.

Martha, for her own part, would have settled for
the least expense and trouble. Immediate cremation
and ashes scattered at sea, with no funeral. But she
presented her thoughts as suggestions and possibilities and gave careful attention to her children's re-
sponses. They agreed about cremation, but for

reasons they found hard to express, they wanted her ashes placed in a nearby cemetery, and they wanted a ceremony—a memorial service of some kind—a ritual of farewell.

They had missed these things after their father died. The arrangements for him were so practical and efficient that their emotional needs had gone unmet. As it happened, their father's ashes had not ever actually been scattered but had been kept in a closet in the son's house, and the children wanted both sets of remains in the same place. Martha agreed. And knew why she agreed. It was what they wanted and needed.

To be as helpful and useful as possible, Martha joined the People's Memorial Society—a cooperative organization that had negotiated a special set of arrangements and fees with an open-minded funeral director. For her membership fee, Martha was given help in filling out forms describing her funeral plans. The society recorded the information necessary for the death certificate and the newspaper obituary. When Martha died, all the family had to do was call the memorial society—they and the funeral director took care of the rest. A great deal of worry and anxiety and confusion were lifted from her family.

—

With her daughter and son, Martha selected and purchased a plot in the cemetery and talked about the funeral service along the way. She gave them

suggestions. Her only insistence was that it be a celebration of life—and that nobody wear black. She
didn't like black, for one thing. And she had read
somewhere that the reason black was the color of
mourning was because in ancient times, people believed that the spirits of the dead could enter the bodies of the living. To keep from being possessed,
mourners disguised themselves by painting their
bodies black or covering themselves with black garments. The custom of women wearing black veils is
an extension of this precaution.

After talking with her doctor and her lawyer, Martha made a Living Will, which prescribed the limits
of care she wanted. She made arrangements with the
Hospice Society regarding home care.

The most difficult discussion revolved around
Martha's desire to die at home and to have some part
in the decision to die when life on the dialysis machine became unbearable for her. She didn't want to
become a financial or emotional burden to her family, and she didn't want to be kept alive by heroic
means. She wanted some say in her demise.

As it turned out, Martha died pretty much as she
wished.

After being bedridden at home for a week, she felt
her time had come and made the decision not to have
any further dialysis. Her children and grandchildren
took turns staying with her, and a visiting nurse came
in every day. Sleep turned into a deep coma, and with

her family gathered around her on April Fool's morning, she took one last breath and passed on.

∽

Martha was lucky. That's what many people said. She had time.

No, that's not it. I think Martha was wise. She *took* time.

Time to think, time to learn, time to consider others.

All of this seems a lot of work.

It's not. Martha put her affairs in order in about a month's time.

If she had not, it would have taken a year out of the lives of her heirs.

Her knowledge made death a compatible reality instead of a fearful enemy.

Her funeral was held on the other side of fear.

How she died was based on how she lived.

Much of what she accomplished can be accomplished by any of us.

Consistently, I have seen that those who take time to plan arrangements with death end up having made new arrangements with life. We all know stories of what happens when people find out they have a limited time to live. Many finally start living well. They simplify their lives, spend time with those they love, slow down, and get around to doing many things they had put off.

What about sudden death, you may ask?

What rituals apply then? When no thought has been given to death?

Death is always expected—always nearby.

Preparing for it is like wearing an existential seat belt.

With forethought you've increased the odds of living through it.

What Martha Carter did was right for her.

It is not what you are supposed to do.

You should do what's right for you and your family.

But you *should* do it.

After they know they are going to die, people often live and die well.

Let me announce, then, to you:

You have a limited time to live.

REVIVAL

The remedy for dirt is soap and water.
The remedy for dying is living.

CHINESE PROVERB

Between the first inhale at birth and the last exhale at death are all the little deaths and revivals. Some part of us is always dying. For an impatient person like me, just waiting—in line or in traffic or on hold—waiting, waiting, waiting . . . is deadly. "I'd rather die than wait."

And I die each night, buried under the coffin cover of darkness.

Only to revive—come to waking life again—at dawn.

When I graduated from school and left home, a world died.

Most of the people I had seen every day, I never saw again, as surely as if they were dead. And the same thing happened when I changed jobs, moved to a new city, or from one part of town to another. The people and places, the habits of a day, the routes to work, the sidewalk scenery, and the framework of a way of life became history—finished, dead. Those who leave their native land to take up life in a new country know about this. As do those who get divorced.

When we've changed our religious views or political convictions, a part of our past dies. When love ends, be it the first mad romance of adolescence, the love that will not sustain a marriage, or the love of failed friendship, it is the same. A death.

Likewise in the event of a miscarriage or an abortion: a possibility is dead. And there is no public or even private funeral. Sometimes only regret and nostalgia mark the passage. And the last rites are held in the solitude of one's most secret self—a service of mourning in the tabernacle of the soul.

Nevertheless, most of us seem to be stubborn about surviving these lesser deaths, finding ways to get up off our knees and get on with it. We fight back—reach out to find new ways and new friends and new places and new reasons for scrambling on. Crossing these thresholds is a rite of passage. Revival is a lifelong ritual.

—

Nothing about being human amazes me more than this capacity for revival.

How dull and meaningless and hopeless life can seem—only to become exciting, vibrant, and filled with hope the next day. Whole nations come back from destruction and oppression—when great problems get addressed and resolved.

All our exits may become entrances.

The human capacity to take whatever life dishes out and to come back is never to be underestimated. How amazing it is, knowing we are all going to die anyhow, that we are so determined to live as well as we can, no matter what. For all our little deaths, we defy our fate and come to life again and again, and yet again. Daily, we redeem ourselves in unspoken rituals of renewal. Daily, we get up and go to work in the construction business of building and repairing and remodeling a life.

The ritual of revival has many names: "born again" and "healing" or simply "getting our act together." Whatever the name, however large or small the act, the urge to reassemble the fragments of our lives into a whole is the same.

∽

Last Sunday afternoon I went through my "drawer ritual."

Restless, with time on my hands and too many things to do on my mind, I paced around the house trying unsuccessfully to get my energy focused. I turned almost unconsciously to "the drawers." Or, as I've come to think of them, the "somewhere drawers," as in, "It's in here somewhere."

Because the space in our houseboat is limited, my wife and I share a small room that serves as a kind of focus for personal life. The room is carefully and clearly divided between us by a long wooden table, and on our respective sides we each have a clothes closet and a chest of drawers.

This common room also serves as the family loading dock—where we leave the baggage we carry back and forth from work: briefcases, books, umbrellas, mail, and coats. In my half, there is an old Japanese tansu chest that I bought because it has many drawers of many sizes and I thought it would keep my possessions and clothes organized. This, and the table beside it, form an L-shaped corner that is my basic life workstation. I dress and undress here, and equip and unequip myself for each day.

Here's what belongs in the series of small drawers at the top of the chest: wallet, keys, spare eyeglasses and sunglasses, gloves, watch, ring, pen and pencil, address book, notepad, small camera, checkbook,

Swiss Army knife, small tape recorder, small tape measure, handkerchiefs, penlight, and small pocket comb. All useful objects. There are several small wicker baskets distributed among the drawers to keep things efficiently ordered and handy.

Impressed?

Don't be.

Over time, in the daily scramble of coming and going, anything small and loose gets dumped higgledy-piggledy into the drawers. All the odds and ends out of pockets and briefcase, and all the bits and pieces that seem to turn up on the table, and all those loose parts that are handed to me by my wife with the comment, ''Here, this is yours, put it somewhere.'' In the ''somewhere'' drawers, of course. Inevitably, there comes the crisis when what I put somewhere is nowhere to be found.

Last Sunday I carefully emptied out all the drawers and laid out the pieces as if they had been found in an archaeological dig. A small-scale museum display of a life. In addition to most of the items listed above that are supposed to be there, I found these:

loose change, matches (both unused and used), Kleenex (ditto), nails, screws, nuts and bolts and washers, miscellaneous mechanical parts of unknown purpose, pipe cleaners, a computer disc, one of my wife's lipsticks, various notes scribbled on scraps of paper, two unmailed letters, three opened rolls of Rolaids, four Chap Sticks (mostly used up), five assorted small batteries, six odd buttons, loose pipe tobacco, one sock, one cuff link, two pencil stubs, refill cartridges for fountain pen and ballpoint pen (used and unused), bicycle wrench, a clothespin, a deck of cards, an unsmoked cigar, a partially smoked cigar, a nail file and toenail clippers, gum wrappers but no gum, used and unused Band-Aids, the corpses of a fly, a moth and two tiny beetly bugs, and a lot of dust and tiny trash.

I kid you not.

But then, you aren't surprised, are you?

Industriously, I washed out the drawers with soap and water, relined them with brown Kraft paper (carefully fitted), and ruthlessly triaged the former contents. Much of it went in the trash can.

A sack of the possibly useful items got dumped into the even bigger drawer in the kitchen. This is called putting things ''somewhere else.'' (Someday, someday, I'll sort that one out.)

Carefully, thoughtfully, I replaced the proper contents in their proper little wicker baskets in their proper drawers and slid the drawers home into their slots in the chest.

There.

The drawer ritual is complete.

My drawers are clean, neat, and worthy of respect.

And on some level, for at least a little while, so is my life.

The ritual of the drawer is deeply satisfying.

Such an accomplishment!

How can something so mundane seem so important?

It has ritual value—as a metaphor of larger designs.

I wonder how many times in my life I have done this?

Often enough to know I will go through this cycle again sometime next year.

Often enough to know this ritual for what it is: not tidying drawers but a symbolic manipulation of the paradoxical nature of my life in general. Order and purpose giving way to disorder and confusion giving way to getting organized again. On a secret level, the ritual of revival.

Even undressing, taking a shower and washing my hair and trimming my beard and filing my nails, and then getting into clean, fresh clothes will suffice sometimes. Same deal. Getting my act together. Revival. Whatever it takes, whatever works to lever the wheels back onto the tracks.

—

This week I am moving my office and studio. From an industrial warehouse where I have been for thirty years to a building in a suburban neighborhood. The difference between the drawer ritual and this move is only a matter of scale. The files and records, the photographs and treasures, the bones and stones and altars. I can't bear to give you the full list—it would fill a book on its own. As it says on the sign in the window of the rug merchant down the street, "Everything Must Go." In the trash, to the Goodwill, or in the moving van. Everything must go. A new era, a clear deck. Until next time.

And I recall other forms this drawer ritual has taken—moving from one job to another, one town to another, one house to another. Moving out of one marriage into another. Moving out of one image of myself into another. Always discarding, repacking, always moving on and at the same time taking some of the accumulated patterns and possessions of a lifetime with me.

What provokes this restless ritual of revision and revival?

A need for meaningful structure, purpose, order in life? Yes.

Boredom, confusion, anxiety? Yes, those, too.

And sometimes sorrow, failure, and fear set us in motion.

"You're fired."

"I want a divorce."

"You have cancer."

"You're an alcoholic."

"She's dead."

"It's over."

We take it. Deal with it. Get on with it.

Cleansing and revival are called for.

And the question now is how to die this death and come to life again.

One of the most remarkable developments in our

culture in the last twenty years is the understanding of the need for community in the process of recovery from these disasters. This is a revival in itself. Support groups, friends, family—other people.

Alcoholics Anonymous and its famed twelve-step program stand out.

It doesn't matter who you are, what your religion or race might be, or your economic status. If you can get to the meeting, stand up and say your name, and say, "I'm an alcoholic," then you've made the first step back. Beyond that come the stages of renewal—centered on exchanging demonic behavior for sacred habits. It's simple, really—we need each other. And have an amazing capacity to assist one another in these rites of passage from death to life again.

Confession and repentance are old rituals.

Every year the Jews observe the Day of Atonement, when they confront their failures and transgressions and sins—and get squared away with God and their families, friends, and neighbors.

Catholics pursue the same end in the confessional with a priest.

Protestant prayers often begin with, "I confess to Almighty God."

In the secular world, we turn to counselors, psychiatrists, and to organized groups of people who have our failings or griefs and our hopes and intentions.

This is the ritual of reconciliation.

It involves the ritual of recognition of damage

done to ourselves and others, the ritual of reunion with the better parts of ourselves, the ritual of reaffirmation of the power of human beings to help one another.

On a daily scale, from an early age we learn a fundamental value of human community: to apologize—to say simply "I'm sorry." And thereby not only to keep our bonds with others intact, but to keep our self-image from the fragmentation caused by anger. A Buddhist would call this the ritual of right action.

෴

I remember being at a summer conference—during an evening lecture.

It was raining buckets outside, and about fifty of us were doing serious business inside, talking about the war in Vietnam—agonizing over our impotence in the face of the horrors of that war.

Suddenly, a very wet, muddy young man burst into the rear of the hall.

"Help me, help me," he cried. He was driving too fast, had missed a turn and spun off the road in the dark, and was himself thrown out onto the road because he was not wearing his seat belt. His pickup truck was hanging on the edge of a ravine. With his wife and child still in it, so scared they couldn't move. "Help me, help me."

As one body we rose and poured out of the hall, running into the rainy night behind the terrified young man. As one we grabbed onto the small truck and pulled it back from the edge, and as one we lifted the truck back onto the road and spun it around onto the shoulder for safety.

The mother and child were in shock, but otherwise uninjured. Tenderly, they were carried back to the conference grounds to someone's room—dried off, wrapped in blankets, comforted. A doctor among us examined them. Warm tea was brewed. Mechanics in the group made sure the truck was in safe working order.

The young man admitted how foolish he had been, how sorry he was to have risked his life and the life of his family, and how deeply he felt our compassion. Within a couple of hours, the young man and his family were on the road again. He will never forget. Nor will those who helped.

This response to crisis—with strangers or friends or family—is part of our nature. Every day, every week, every year since time began, whatever the size or nature of the crisis, this has been true of the human community. A fact that must be laid alongside all we know of the horror of man's inhumanity to man. Few of us do not have a story to tell—of what we gave or what was given to us in response to "Help me, help me." We are capable of being agents of one another's revival. None of us can go all the way alone.

Even in the midst of the unbearable agonies of prisons and concentration camps, there are those who choose to help—to give to others: bread, shoes, comfort, whatever. These acts of compassion are the shining, diamond-tough confirmations of human dignity. This is keeping our affairs in order at the highest level. This is communion in its highest form. The ritual of the keeping of the living flame. Held daily in the unfinished cathedral of the human spirit.

∽

Crossing the threshold between being a self-concerned child and being an other-concerned adult is a death-and-rebirth transformation. A major rite of passage.

When did you first realize you were an adult?

When did you realize you had grown up?

—

One man's answer:

"I knew I had become an adult when I realized I had a conscience."

A teacher's story. Daniel, now fifty-seven. In March of 1965, he got a phone call from a friend, asking him to come as soon as possible to Selma, Alabama.

Daniel knows now how crucial to the success of the civil-rights movement the confrontation taking place in the little Alabama town was. But when he got the phone call to come and help swell the ranks of marchers, he did not want to go. He believed in civil rights in a vague way, and believed that sooner or later it would come, but this wasn't his fight. He was a white Southerner living in the Far West, and he didn't want to become an "outside agitator."

Also, his mother and father would never forgive him if he went to Selma.

Besides that, he was young, working two jobs, with a young family, and he didn't have the time or money to go. Even more, he was afraid—scared to death of getting beaten up or even killed. One man had just been beaten to death just for being there—a young white man like himself. No way was he going to Selma, Alabama. No reasonable man in his situation would go. He was no hero.

But something in his soul—in his heart, in his mind—kept him awake all night. And the next morning he explained how he felt to his wife. He thought he should at least go and see firsthand, and make up his mind what to do when he got there.

Respectably dressed in suit and tie, he drove in a rented car from the Birmingham airport to the edge of the town and walked to the area of the confrontation, there in the middle of a street.

On one side were the representatives of law and order—police, state troopers, sheriffs, and government authorities in plainclothes, plus a huge crowd of white people. They were determined to block the protest march any way they could. Daniel knew people like these; he had grown up with them. He didn't stand out among them—he was one of them.

Opposite the police line was a street filled with singing, chanting Negroes—and mixed in among them he could see white people. He was surprised to notice that some were priests and nuns. He didn't see many people like himself over there.

On his side of the line, there were rage, weapons, authority, and the threat of violence—fueled by the fear of change. This side vented feelings with curses. On the other side, there was singing—and the presence of the unyielding force of self-determination. They sang "We Shall Overcome."

He remembered the final phrase from the "Pledge of Allegiance"—a pledge he had been taught on the first day of school: ". . . with liberty and justice for all."

Maybe it *was* his fight. Becoming just one more private soldier in this war wouldn't make all that much difference to the civil-rights movement, but it would make a huge difference in who he was or was not going to be for the rest of his life. Adults did the hard stuff and didn't turn away when things got scary. He knew that if he crossed this line, life would never be quite the same.

He thought about his children and his children's children.

The marchers sang, "Which side are you on?"

And he knew.

Making a big circle through the adjacent residential area, he found a way to cross over the line and a place to stand. He began to sing.

◌

Rituals and rites of passage often take place where words cannot go—in a solitary, secret inner kingdom where just knowing is enough. We experience and understand changes we cannot articulate. And need not. Which is why we often say at crucial times in life, "I don't know what to say," or "I just can't tell you how much I . . ." and "Words fail me." Human language—our metaphors and analogies and rational expressions—often are a poor substitute for the most profound level of knowledge. The rituals of renewal and revival regularly take place in silence.

Wordiness often ruins public rituals. The verbal waterfall drowns the private sounds in the minds of those in attendance. It is not true that if we get all the words just right, the occasion will be right. A successful rite of passage must leave room for the eloquence of silence.

Silence is always part of great music.
Silence is always part of great art.
Silence is always part of a great life.

–

The Society of Friends—the Quakers—understand and practice this. They meet and celebrate in silence, knowing silence often speaks louder than words.

A Quaker wedding is a case in point.

As in all their habits of worship, Quakers' weddings are simple affairs. In the most traditional

Quaker services, there are no words, no music, no complicated ceremony or fuss-and-bother. The bride and groom gather with their families, friends, special guests, and the members of the religious community.

It is a service of worship.

In solemn silence, they sit together until a communal feeling of consensus and affirmation has been achieved. When the spirit moves them, they rise together, and the couple is married. All present sign the wedding certificate. A reception follows, and now there is time for talk.

While this may seem an extremely austere way to wed, one is mindful of what's at the heart of a wedding: the hearts of the couple involved. Sometimes words and ceremony and other people get in the way of what needs to be done.

One does not have to be a Quaker to put this wisdom to good use.

—

I remember well a couple who came to me wanting to be married in the Quaker spirit. Both were attorneys working in the same office. The land mines and complications in their lives and the lives of their families rivaled anything I had ever encountered. Parental acts of incest, violent abuse, and alcoholic rage scarred the childhoods of both of them. Though both had overcome difficult personal problems, the bitterness and pain connected to family were unresolved. Which meant that great bitterness and pain could come to their wedding if their families were involved. It just could not be a family affair for them. As they poured out the grief, I could understand and agree with their decision. They had buried the past—and now needed a revival of hope for family life in the future.

Sometimes things are just as bad as they seem.

Why not just live together? No. They wanted a ceremony—something to confirm their relationship in the eyes of the world; they wanted to be husband and wife—to have a wedding. And they wanted witnesses. A civil service with a judge wouldn't do. They'd already spent too much time in courts of law and were tired of words. They wanted the minimum ceremony—with the maximum meaning.

After researching what was legally required and talking with me about what was spiritually necessary, they began to know what should happen. We conferred several times over several months. There was no hurry. I was moved by the depth of their caring for one another. If this process of negotiation is the real wedding, then I sensed a powerful and lasting relationship in the making.

—

Just after dawn on a warm, wet September Sunday morning, the bride and groom, their two closest friends, and I drove to a large woodland park. Shielded from the dripping sky by raincoats and umbrellas, we walked together through ranks of ancient fir trees on a path along the edge of a cliff overlooking Puget Sound. The couple had often walked there and often stopped at one particular clearing to look at the waves below and the mountains in the far distance.

They asked the witnesses and me to stand close enough to see but far enough away so as not to impose a presence. Saying they would be back when they were married, they gave their raincoats and umbrella to their witnesses and walked off hand in hand in the rain, finally standing some distance away at their chosen place. The soft sound of the rain dripping down through the trees was the wedding march.

We saw them stop and turn to look at one another without touching. Then, standing side by side, they put their arms around each other's waists and looked toward the sea and the mountains for a long time. She leaned her head on his shoulder, and he leaned his head on hers.

They turned and held each other in a lingering embrace. They kissed in a most tender way. Laughing, he picked her up in his arms and swung her around in a circle. Carefully, he returned her to her feet, and with arms around each other, they walked back to us, smiling in silence—a silence too fine to break until we got back to our cars, when she announced, "We're married now."

Later, in a coffee shop over breakfast, we dried out and signed the legal papers. When he asked, "What do we owe you?" I had to say I was in their debt for the meaning their wedding had for me. In keeping my mouth shut, I had contributed to one of the finest weddings ever. It revived my own belief in what human beings can accomplish together.

In the months leading up to their wedding day, they had said everything that needed to be said. When they crossed the threshold together into marriage, they needed no words. They knew why they were there, they knew what they had promised, they knew where they were going. Since God is everywhere, they felt married in the presence of God, as well. Despite saying nothing in the ceremony, they had still promised each other everything. Their covenant was made in that place where words cannot ever go. I've no doubt they did the right thing. It may have been the most eloquent ceremony I have attended.

—

Interestingly enough, the bride and groom asked the witnesses and me not to tell anyone of their marriage, because they wanted to enjoy this occasion between the two of them for a while. I notice this often happens when a couple becomes pregnant—they keep the news to themselves for a time. Celebrations may be deep without being wide.

The couple didn't leave out the noisy part of the celebration—it just happened at another time. There is a time for silence and a time for Whoopee. In October, the couple threw a costume party—on Halloween, when demons are traditionally exorcised—an auspicious decision, given what I knew about the couple's past.

In the middle of the party, the couple announced

their marriage. I was otherwise engaged that night and couldn't go. I heard the groom was disguised as Lazarus the day after he came back to life, and the bride came as Sleeping Beauty, the day after she woke up. How appropriate—certainly their marriage had revived hopes of finally having a family life they could believe in.

I see one or the other of them once in a while. They've been married almost seventeen years now. They've a couple of lively kids, a home, and all the rest that goes with it, I suppose. I suspect if I checked the site of their wedding on their anniversary, I'd find them there, rain or shine, reviving and reaffirming their vows in care-full silence.

New Year's, Valentine's Day, Passover, Easter, Memorial Day, Fourth of July, and on through Thanksgiving and Christmas. These annual occasions have been thoroughly and exhaustively examined in countless books and articles. These public holidays have become commercial events having little to do with the seasons of my private and secret life.

For many of us, the new year—that season of new beginnings—does not begin on January 1. New Year's Day is a name on a calendar marking the end of the craziness of Christmas. Most of us go to bed early on New Year's Eve and stay in bed late the next morning because there really isn't much we're supposed to do. "Do Nothing Day" is a better name for it. And we can use a Do Nothing Day, that's for sure. It's a break, not a beginning.

For some, December 21 marks the new year—the day on which the longest night is passed and the earth turns toward light again. For Jews, the New Year begins in the fall, at harvesttime, marking the completion of a cycle of birth, growth, and death.

For all of us, during the years we were in school—and for all those involved in education now—the new year begins after Labor Day when classes resume. When we say, "This year I'm going to do better," we mean when school starts.

For a huge portion of the population in the world

of manufacturing and wholesale distribution, the new year starts immediately after a major season is over. The developing, designing, and distribution of products has a huge lead time. As I write in early summer, for example, the production of Christmas decorations, advertising, and sales is in full swing. Poinsettias are being planted in greenhouses. The tsunami wave of selling has already been shaken into motion.

The diversity of our culture and our economy and our ways of life means our seasonal pattern has changed from largely rural and agricultural to largely urban and technological.

Yet for every one of us, there is still an annual cycle of personal seasons.

A productive time and a fallow time.

A time to generate new ideas and a time to make them work.

A time to invest and a time to sell.

A time to get organized and a time to let go.

A time to get in shape and a time to be lazy.

This paradoxical swing of the rhythmic pendulum of life is not to be ignored or disallowed. It is the swinging of the pendulum that drives the clock. My year begins in the fall, with the rise of the Harvest Moon. I give presents and celebrate people when I feel like it. April Fool's Day is my personal holiday. And the first snow means winter. So it goes with me, never mind what's happening in the stores.

My daily life is likewise a matter of idiosyncratic style.

I know I'm most creatively productive between six A.M. and noon, and for about fifty minutes at a time. Then I must stop and do something nonmental for a little while. I know if I skip breakfast, I will regret it in the afternoon, when I run out of energy. I know I work well under high pressure but know I need times of doing nothing. I know if I take breaks during the day, I will accomplish just as much as if I worked straight through. A nap is essential. I know if I don't get enough sleep, the lamp of my life burns low. I know I feel compelled to rise with the first light of day, which means getting up very early in summer and late in winter. My life is more driven by daylight than by calendars. I do not think I am unique in this.

Awareness of these inner rhythms and private seasons is not provided by business or culture, but only by being mindful of what makes a life go well and respecting that knowledge.

I remember a "Peanuts" cartoon in which Charlie Brown is complaining to Linus about his lunch because it has the same thing in it every day. When Linus asks Charlie Brown who makes his lunch, Charlie Brown says, "I do."

When it comes to the rituals of my life, I make my own lunch.

If the rituals do not work, they may be re-formed.

Whatever and whenever the public celebrations

may be, I live my life in tune with private and secret rhythms as personal as my pulse. The same is true for everyone I know. Our lives are endless ritual. The patterns that give meaningful shape to the day, the year, and the life are sacred to me, and to us all.

We began with Alice's story—with the rituals of the first hour of an ordinary day. It seems appropriate to complete a circle and tell you Sam's story—about the rituals of day's end. In the middle years of their lives, both Alice and Sam have come to understand how the patterns of these short hours illuminate the patterns of a week and a year and a lifetime. The wisdom of Alice and Sam is elemental: the Holy Sacraments are made out of the Daily Stuff.

Sam lives in my neighborhood. Suffice it to say that he is in late middle age—he's been around. What he looks like and what he does for a living are not important. It's how he thinks and what he does to make living worthwhile that are impressive. As with Alice, you probably know someone like him. As with Alice, you may even *be* someone like him.

Almost every evening I see him walking both his old dog and a recently acquired puppy. It's a common scene—an ordinary event in most neighborhoods. You can almost set your clock by his reliable rhythm—coming by at ten and going back by at ten-thirty. Winter, summer, spring, and fall. Rain or snow, clouds or starshine, he walks the dogs.

Nothing dramatic here—a regular guy and regular dogs taking a regular walk. Out walking myself, I followed him at a distance a couple of times. His dogs pause to do their business, but he also has reason to pause. The dogs look for a tree, and Sam looks for stars.

I spoke to him about this.

He said the dogs keep him doing something important for himself. The old dog finds his leash each evening and stands by the door, waiting. The old dog is driven by his lower intestine and bladder. The young dog frolics through the house, yapping and wriggling, driven by enthusiasm for any opportunity for action and adventure. But Sam is compelled by a need for what he tells his wife is "some fresh air." Whatever he calls it, she understands where he is going and why. While he is out of the house, she will do the dishes. For the same reasons, he goes out with the dogs. It is a sacred habit—a reflective time alone.

Sam says that on these walks he settles the affairs of the day and thinks about tomorrow. He calms down from the busyness of his life, notices the weather, the seasons, the trees, and the stars, and thinks about "all the big stuff."

He has watched the essential evening news of this turning and evolving world and is ready for bed and sleep. "Harmony" is a word that comes to mind.

Sam knows the old dog will not live much longer, so the young dog is there to overlap the inevitable loss. He thinks the young dog will learn a lot from the older dog he can't learn from people. And buying the young dog is an acknowledgment of life and death and a gesture toward the future—of Sam's continuing to be around for a while himself.

When my neighbor walks the dogs, he performs a ritual act of *sacra simplicitas,* to use the church Latin: "sacred simplicity." Walking the dog is in truth a ritual of renewal and revival on an intimate scale—a small rebirth of well-being on a daily basis.

Several years ago, Sam spent weeks at the bedside of a close friend who was dying of cancer. A man who had many regrets. He said if he had only known death was so near, he would not have hurried to meet it. When asked what he would have done differently, he thought for a long time and said something surprising: For one thing, he would have taken time to walk his dog.

—

There is, indeed, a time for all things under heaven.
And for all the great rites of passage;
Weddings and funerals, graduations and
    retirements.
A time for anniversaries and reunions;
For sunrise and sundown, for moon and rain, for
    stars.
A time for the first breath—"ah"—and the last
    breath—"oh."
But in the meantime, there is the infinite moment—
A time to do the dishes,
And a time to walk the dog.

CODA

January 2, 1995

A friend who is an avid spelunker—an explorer of caves—told me of running out of time for exploring underground just as he had shined his headlight into a passage beyond which he could see a fascinating and as yet unexplored chamber with even more passages leading off in many directions. How frustrating! Still, he had the satisfaction of knowing he had something to look forward to another time.

So it is with me and the subject of rituals.

Deadlines happen. Explorations end. And this writing must be sent off today to be shaped by the substantial skills of those who turn pages of words into bound books. My mood is one of affirmative frustration. Yes, this rituals book is done. But I've enough unexpressed thoughts and experiences to double its size.

In part, the blame for my condition may be gratefully laid at the doorstep of the more than three hundred people who have read and contributed to this manuscript in its many stages of development. Each person suggested something I had overlooked. Each person had experienced rites of passage I had not mentioned. And each had meaningful life rituals unknown to me. Instead of just providing a constructive critique of what I had written, many pointed me down paths I had not walked before, where I discovered other species of ritual. Here are just a few of the comments that could have led to another chapter in this book:

What about ritual gestures of blessing and insult?

How about the rituals of academic communities?

Why not talk about baby showers, men's poker groups, and other gender-separation rituals?

Aren't some rituals harmful or intended to be?

When does a ritual become a counterproductive obsession?

How about including an actual ritual of renewal for marriage?

And a housewarming ceremony and family table blessings?

How about other kinds of funeral services for unique circumstances?

How about the rituals of politics—what's sacred about them?

I will consider this book successful if you finish it in the same spirit: wanting to tell me all you know that I clearly do not, and suggesting items to cover next time.

It's a good thing I didn't set out to write the definitive book on rituals and rites of passage. Nobody can possibly have the last word. What I've written is a guide to the landscape I know with a compilation of the judgments I have made out of my experience. How I wish I could hear or read your response.

—

This book has engendered a new ritual of my own.

From time to time, I pay my respects at my final resting place.

Visiting my own grave has become a ritual for me—a sacred habit.

Recently, I noticed the names on the nearest graves: Grimm and Pleasant.

Being buried between Grimm and Pleasant has a poetic rightness about it.

Visiting my grave has the reliable capacity to untwist the snarls in my mind and soul, especially when I get angry about small things or lose track of what's important. On one visit, I realized that if I died that day and my wife were to put an honest epitaph on my headstone, it would say, "Here lies a jackass—too pissed off to live long."

How I'd hate to die mad.

Once I went up to the cemetery late at night. Bringing my favorite blanket with me—a faded red wool Hudson's Bay blanket—I lay down on it on my grave in a man-in-the-coffin position. I closed my eyes and thought about how being dead is just going to sleep and not waking up. I opened my eyes and was startled. This gravesite has an incredible view— looking straight up, I could see starshine that comes to me from millions of light-years away.

Looking up and trying to conceive of the magnitude and complexity of space, I was caught between two overwhelming thoughts: that there may be no other intelligent life out there or that the number of worlds occupied by life like us may well be infinite. Either point of view staggers my mind. Just being able to consider such questions is amazing enough.

I have never liked the phrase that says we're just made of dust and return to dust. We are energy, which is interchangeable with light. We are fire and water and earth. We are air and atoms and quarks. Moreover, we are dreams, hopes, and fears held together by wisdom and driven apart by folly. So much more than dust. The biblical verse should say, "Miracle thou art and to Mystery returneth."

The light I see from my grave started toward me before I came into being.

The source of the light may have died out by now.

That's a scientific fact.

My life gives off another kind of light as it consumes its energy.

That light may shine long after the source is gone.

That's a statement of poetry and intention.

Light is both constant and relative.

–

A friend of mine is a juggler. He's good—really good. He doesn't juggle spectacular objects—no flaming torches or running chain saws. Just balls. He's intent on doing the simplest thing as well as possible. He can juggle eight balls and keeps trying for nine, which would tie the world's record. I can juggle two balls and sometimes three, so I know just enough to know how really spectacular his achievement is.

Once I asked him this question: If I were in your class, what would I appreciate about your ability? Or in other words, what would another highly accomplished juggler know about your skills that I miss because I'm just an awed amateur?

He said that the average spectator was impressed that he could catch so many things and throw them up again. The truth is that the hardest parts are holding the balls just right, throwing them one at a time in rhythm, and not altering your breathing or inner adrenaline level as the number of balls increases. Also, an expert would notice he had developed and learned to trust a reliable pattern of movements—a pattern that includes missing a ball sometimes. When you miss, you don't get upset or quit—it's then that the champion juggler does not blow his cool or change his inner state.

The secret of juggling is inner harmony and knowing how to let go.

There's a philosophy of life in that statement.

As I learn to juggle the parts of my life, I have come to understand that meaningful rituals have a lot to do with gaining that inner harmony and making letting go as much a part of life as holding on.

Rituals anchor us to a center while freeing us to move on and confront the everlasting unpredictability of life. The paradox of ritual patterns and sacred habits is that they simultaneously serve as solid footing and springboard, providing a stable dynamic in our lives.

෨෨

Rituals of hello and good-bye are basic to all relationships between people.

"Hello. How are you? Well, hello. Fine, how're you? Just fine, thank you."

"So long. Take care. Keep in touch. Let's get together. See you soon."

These entrance and exit lines are a part of our daily onstage life.

I like hellos. I'm a hello enthusiast.

When I travel and have time on my hands at airports, I sometimes stand in the middle of the arrival lounge, where people are awaiting passengers from an incoming plane. It's exciting being around people carrying welcoming signs and flowers. Romantic to see the spruced-up lover come to meet the lovee. And heartwarming to be near family reunions.

The joyous cries of hellos are infectious. "Here she comes!"—"Daddy, Daddy"—"It's him!"— "Bill! Mary! Over here!"—"Grandma, Grandma!"—"Welcome back! Welcome home! It's so good to see you!"

I like all the laughing and hugging and kissing and excitement. More than once I've caught myself just before I hugged a perfect stranger. It's a little weird being really glad to see someone you've never met. The rituals of reunion are contagious.

Exits and farewells are not so easy. I don't hang around the departure lounges at airports. I hate good-byes. I am not good at them.

So it is with the end of a book. I've spent time thinking about you, and you've spent time thinking about me, but not in the same place and time. It's even harder saying farewell to someone I've met only in my imagination. I've missed you.

If you've come this far in this book, I thank you for the company we've kept and hope that I see you in person sometime—perhaps in the arrival lounge at an airport—and that you feel like saying hello. After the ritual of meeting, we can pick up where we began: "From beginning to end, the rituals of our lives . . ."

REFERENCES
AND
RESOURCES

This section combines the purposes of appendix, bibliography, footnotes, and index, while avoiding their formal mechanical constraints.

Above all, my intention is to be useful in a practical and personal way.

Each entry must have passed these tests:

1. I have personally read and made use of the material.
2. I would personally recommend the material to you.
3. The material is readily available.

The resource material is organized by chapter but applies almost entirely to the sections on weddings, funerals, and birth celebrations.

All references are annotated.

Finding that some of my best illustrative anecdotes have already appeared in previous books, I have taken the liberty of referring to those stories as a way of jogging your memory if you have read them or else suggesting you will find a chapter in this book expanded by adding this material.

∾

REFERENCES

References to stories previously appearing in books by Robert Fulghum, all published by Villard/Random House in hardback and Ballantine/Ivy in paperback, the last three also available in Random House Large Print editions.

All I Really Need to Know I Learned in Kindergarten (1988 and 1990)

It Was on Fire When I Lay Down on It (1989 and 1991)
Uh-Oh (1991 and 1993)
Maybe (Maybe Not) (1993 and 1994)
(Page numbers vary slightly among the hardcover, paper-back, and large print editions.)

–

Beginning

For the opposite way of beginning a day, see the story of the man with the briefcase in *Uh-Oh* on pp. 153 ff. (pp. 155 ff. in paperback and pp. 161 ff. in the large print edition).

Propositions

For an expansion of the notion of the secret life, see pp. 7 ff. in *Maybe (Maybe Not),* and the piece about confessions in the same book, p. 13 in the hardcover and paperback and p. 15 in the large print edition.

A Cemetery View

For a description of the bench in this cemetery, see the story beginning on p. 209 (p. 229 in the large print edition) in *It Was on Fire When I Lay Down on It.*

Once

See p. 75 (p. 81 in the large print edition) in *Uh-Oh* about learning to play with fire.

Reunion

The Thanksgiving story beginning on p. 131 (p. 145 in the large print edition) in the *Fire* book applies. And see the story about hide-and-seek in the *Kindergarten* book, p. 56.

Union

My all-time favorite wedding story about the Mother of the Bride begins on p. 9 in the *Fire* book, and my second-favorite wedding story begins on p. 135 (p. 151 in the large print edition)—about a mixed marriage. And my third-favorite wedding story is also in the same book—p. 145 (p. 163 in the large print edition)—about a second marriage in later years.

Born

See p. 39 (p. 43 in the large print edition) in *Maybe (Maybe Not)* for a story about conception, which connects to the adoption story in this book about rituals.

Dead

P. 173 (p. 181 in the large print edition) in *Uh-Oh* for the funniest funeral story I know, and p. 147 (p. 155 in the large print edition) in the same book for a story about the funeral of a dog.

Revival

In *Uh-Oh,* on p. 115, (p. 119 in the large print edition), there is an expanded view of the idea of a new year, and a story about coming back from suicide begins on p. 99 (p. 111 of the large print edition) in *Maybe.*

Coda

See p. 215 (p. 235 in the large print edition) in *Fire* for thoughts on the end of a book and a day and a life.

෨෧

RESOURCES

Once—The First Time

1. *The First Time,* by Karen Bouris, published in 1993 by Conari Press.

   Subtitled *Women Speak Out About "Losing Their Vir-*

ginity,'' and therefore meaningful in its own right for women, this is a book every man should read. It covers a subject on which I was almost completely ignorant, and it left me informed and enlightened and empathetic. As far as I know, this is the most forthright treatment of the sexual initiation of women in our society. Bouris, by the way, is the co-author of another groundbreaking book I admire: *Random Acts of Kindness.*

2. *The Ordinary Is Extraordinary,* by Amy Laura Dombro and Leah Wallach, published in 1988 by Simon and Schuster.

   The best description I've found on how ordinary daily routines become sacred rituals for children under the age of three. Practical and spiritual at the same time. I would give this book to children when they have children of their own.

   –

Union—Weddings

There is more material available regarding weddings than any other rite of passage. Every bookstore has a section devoted to the occasion, with a substantial number of books from which to choose. Many have merit, depending on your particular style and need. I find five worthy of special mention:

1. *There's No Such Thing as a Perfect Wedding* by Margaret Bigger, published in 1991 by Down Home Press, P.O. Box 4126, Asheboro, N.C. 27204, now in its seventh printing and available in most bookstores.

   Wedding celebrations need laughter. This book is a collection of true wedding tales illustrating all the crazy, stupid, funny, and disastrous dimensions of getting married. Hilarious. Great material for the rehearsal-dinner speeches.

2. *Into the Garden, a Wedding Anthology,* edited by Robert

Hass and Stephen Mitchell, published in 1993 by Harper-Collins.

The best collection of poetry and prose on love and marriage I've seen. Broad and wide and deep in the quality of selections. Inspirational reading in and for itself, and very useful as a resource for wedding-service materials.

3. *Weddings / A Complete Guide to All Religious and Interfaith Marriage Services,* by Abraham Klausner, published in 1986 by Signet Books.

I use this book each time I perform a mixed marriage. Informative, accurate, and useful. The writer combines knowledge and wisdom in a nonjudgmental view of both the specifics and universals in marriage ceremonies. I especially like his Service of Renewal found at the end of the book.

4. *The Groom's Survival Manual,* by Michael Perry, published in 1991 by Pocket Books, and *A Groom of One's Own,* by Mimi Pond, published in 1993 by Penguin Books.

These are the only two books I can recommend that are written for the groom—everything else is written primarily with the bride in mind. These two books are both written with an irreverent sense of humor, as well as with a realistic view of the place of the groom in a wedding. Laughter is a life raft when the raging sea of matrimonial planning seems about to swamp the ship.

–

Born—Celebrations of Family and Community

1. *New Traditions,* by Susan Abel Lieberman, published in 1991 by HarperCollins.

Among many, many books describing ways to create or revive rituals of celebration in a family setting, this is the only one that has a ring of practicality about it, speaking as it does out of examples of what people have actually done, as opposed to a position that suggests an ideal of what you should do. I have purchased and given away a couple dozen of these books in response to the request to "give me some good examples of contemporary family rituals that work." This book makes a fine gift to new parents.

—

Dead—Funerals, Memorial Services, Getting Affairs in Order

There is more material here than on any other chapter in this book, because the resource materials are not readily accessible in any one place in a bookstore, and are not reviewed for quality or usefulness in any source I've seen.

1. *Affairs in Order,* by Patricia Anderson, published in 1991 by Collier/Macmillan—1993 in paperback edition.

   The single most useful and complete resource guide to all matters pertaining to death and dying. If what you need to know is not in this book, it tells you where and how to find it. This is one of the best reference books I've ever seen on any subject. It has a permanent place on my shelf of important books and is a gift I give to personal friends. I not only recommend you buy it and read it, I urge you to do so.

2. *The Last Dance,* by Lynne Ann Despelder and Albert Lee Strickland, third edition, published in 1992 by Mayfield Publishing Company.

   Designed as a text for a college-level course on death and dying, it is a paradigm of a superb teaching tool as well as the best available text on the subject. Approaches death and dying from the perspective of history, ethics, religion, cultural anthropology, the law, physiology, politics, and literature. Nobody should consider his or her education complete without the information in this book. You can take the course by reading the text.

3. *The Hospice Handbook* by Larry Beresford, published in 1993 by Little, Brown and Company—in paperback.

   The best single source for information about hospice care during terminal illness—the where, how, why, and when are all spelled out clearly. Excellent references and resources section at the end of the book.

4. *How to Embalm Your Mother-in-Law,* by Robert T. Hatch—a Citadel Press Book published by Carol Publishing Group in 1993—paperback.

   How could I pass up a book with a title like that? I found it really contains a serious account of what happens to a human body from the time of death until burial—information that is difficult to get from undertakers. Once you read the straightforward description of the embalming process, you will wonder why people would want such a thing done to their own corpse or the body of anyone they loved and respected.

5. *Necessary Losses,* by Judith Viorst, published in paperback in 1987 by Fawcett/Ballantine.

   The subtitle was enough to turn me off: *The Loves, Illusions, Dependencies, and Impossible Expectations That All of Us Have to Give Up in Order to Grow.* But someone kept insisting I read this book, and I found it was not another self-help manual, but an honest description of the inevitable letting go of many sorts that makes going on with life and into death possible. Again, this is a book I often give as a present to someone trying to stay afloat and swim in deep waters.

6. *The High Cost of Dying* by Gregory W. Young, published in paperback in 1994 by Prometheus Books.

   This slim volume is an excellent guide to funeral planning—the one you will wish you had read before you had to plan a funeral, rather than afterward. If it had been available years ago, I would have routinely given it to any family who asked my professional help in preparing for a funeral.

7. *The Art of Condolence,* by Leonard M. Zunin and Hilary Stanton Zunin, published in paperback in 1991 by Harper Perennial, a division of HarperCollins.

"What to write, what to say, what to do at a time of loss." I wish I had written this book. I do take its excellent advice and suggestions to heart. Not only does it cover a difficult and sensitive subject thoughtfully, but it is well written. Exceptionally useful appendix.

The following pages are forms I used when putting my affairs in order through the People's Memorial Society.

Forward to Funeral Home - please complete both sides

PUTTING MY HOUSE IN ORDER

INFORMATION FOR FUNERAL HOME

This is to notify the contracting morturary of my wishes regarding disposal of my remains

Do not hesitate to consult your religious leader or funeral director for guidance in completing this form, if you wish. Print the word or words necessary to complete the statements to express your wishes and provide the additional information requested.

Name _____ PMA number _____

It is my wish that my remains be _____
cremated, buried, entombed

It is my wish that the ashes be _____
(Funeral Director will be responsible   scattered, buried, given to next of kin, executor (personal representative) or friend
for storage of ashes for 2 months only)

If burial preferred, cemetery arrangements _____ made. If already arranged,
should be, have been

fill in: _____
name of cemetery   city or place of cemetery   section   plot

I _____ want a service. If a service is held, prefer _____
do, do not   *memorial or funeral

If a service is held, I would like it held in a _____ church, mortuary chapel, residence, (other place-please state)

If a church is preferred, give: _____ / _____ / _____ / _____
name of church / address of church / city or place / postal code

I _____ want newspaper notices published.
   do, do not

I _____ prefer memorial gifts in lieu of flowers. If memorial gifts in lieu of flowers pre-
   do, do not
ferred, I would request that donations be sent to the following organization:

_____ / _____ / _____ / _____
name of organization or charity / street address / city or place / postal code

I _____ wish to donate my eyes, at time of death, to the eye bank.
   do, do not

I _____ wish to donate such other organs, bone or tissue, at the time of death as may be
   do, do not
considered medically useful. This also authorizes donations of pace maker, if applicable.

I _____ wish to donate my body, at time of death, to closest Medical Teaching Facility.
   do, do not

_____ / _____
name of next of kin, or executor, to indicate his/herknowledge / signature of member
and approval of plan.

_____ / _____
relationship of above to member / date

_____ / _____ / _____
next of kin or executor's street address / city / state

*Memorial Service without the deceased present - Funeral Service with deceased present.

314

VITAL STATISTICS

All the information on this page is required by the State Registrar of Vital Statistics

(Please Print)   Date _____ 19 __

Your name _____
　　　　　first　　　　　middle　　　　　last

Your street address _____
　　　　　city　　　　　state　　　　　zip code

Mailing Address _____

Your Marital status _____ single, married, widowed or divorced

If married, widowed, or divorced;

give _____
　all given names of husband in full

or _____
　all given names of wife in full　　　　maiden name

Your Occupation (a) _____
　　Kind of business or industry in which worked (if retired, give former)

　　(b) _____
　　kind of work done during most of working life

Your birthday _____ Age _____
　month (by name)　date　year　　　　at last birthday

Your birthplace _____
city   state

Your Father's name _____
first   middle   last

Your Mother's name _____
first   middle   maiden name

Your Sex _____   Race _____

Your Next of kin _____
name   street address   city or place   zip code   phone #

Your Social Security Number _____

Your Doctor _____
name   street address   city or place   zip code   phone #

Military Service _____
yes/no   rate or rank   branch   serial number

VA claim no _____   place and date of entry   place and date of discharge

High school Graduate _____   College or University Years Completed _____
yes/no

Resided in County Since _____

Smoked in Past 15 Years _____
yes/no

Hispanic _____
yes/no

PLEASE KEEP THIS PAGE

PUTTING MY HOUSE IN ORDER

Information for Family, Executor, and Friends (Personal Representative)

Please complete both sides

This is to notify my family, executor, and close friends of my wishes regarding the disposal of my remains and the following arrangements that have been made through

THE PEOPLES MEMORIAL ASSOCIATION, INC. OF SEATTLE, WASHINGTON

To fulfill my wishes and complete these arrangements when my death occurs, please notify

_____
NAME OF FUNERAL HOME

_____
PHONE NUMBER

Do not hesitate to consult your religious leader or funeral director for guidance in completing this form, if you wish. Print the word or words necessary to complete the statements to express your wishes and provide the additional information requested.

Name _____ PMA number _____

It is my wish that my remains be _____ cremated, buried, entombed

It is my wish that the ashes be _____ scattered, buried, given to next of kin, executor (personal representative) or friend
(Funeral Director will be responsible for storage of ashes for 2 months only)

If burial preferred, cemetery arrangements _____ should be, have been _____ made. If already arranged,

fill in: _____   _____   _____   _____
        name of cemetery   city or place of cemetery   section   plot

I _____ want a service. If a service is held, prefer _____ *memorial or funeral
  do, do not

If a service is held, I would like it held in a _____ church, mortuary chapel, residence, (other place-please state)

If a church is preferred, give:

	name of church	address of church	city or place	postal code

I _____ want newspaper notices published.
   do, do not

I _____ prefer memorial gifts in lieu of flowers. If memorial gifts in lieu of flowers pre-
   do, do not

ferred. I would request that donations be sent to the following organization:

	name of organization or charity	street address	city or place	postal code

I _____ wish to donate my eyes, at time of death, to the eye bank.
   do, do not

I _____ wish to donate such other organs, bone or tissue, at the time of death as may be
   do, do not

considered medically useful. This also authorizes donations of pace maker, if applicable.

I _____ wish to donate my body, at time of death, to closest Medical Teaching Facility.
   do, do not

_____   _____
name of next of kin, or executor, to indicate his/herknowledge   signature of member
and approval of plan.

_____   _____
relationship of above to member   date

_____   _____
next of kin or executor's street address   city   state

*Memorial Service without the deceased present - Funeral Service with deceased present.

Keep this section with your personal papers for use by your survivors.

Location of my will _____

Location of Insurance Policies _____

Executor (personal representative) named _____

My Attorney is _____

I have Bank Accounts at _____ location _____ acct.#

_____ location _____ acct.#

_____ location _____ acct.#

Safety Deposit Box Numbers _____ Banks _____

Location of Safety Deposit Box Key _____

Real Estate Owned _____

_____

_____

_____

_____

Location of Deeds

I have the following stocks, bonds, contracts or other valuables at:

My social security number

Other information

Signature

Address

My phone is

Date compiled
(change as revised)

320

DISPOSITION AUTHORIZATION
(Decedent During Lifetime)

1.   I declare that it is my wish and I hereby authorize and direct that, upon

my death, my remains be _____.
                              (Write either the word "CREMATED" or "INTERRED")
If I have written the word "CREMATED" above, I further direct that my cremated
remains be disposed of as follows:

_____

2.   Further, I direct that all of my relatives, surviving at my death, honor this
authorization.

3.   I direct that no funeral home, cemetery and/or cremation authority shall
be liable for arranging for or undertaking the disposition of my remains if done in
reliance on this authorization.

4. Further, I direct that my estate, heirs, legal and personal representatives, at their sole expense, shall defend, hold harmless, and indemnify any such funeral home, cemetery and/or cremation authority from any claim, liability, suit, cause of action, cost, or expense (including without limitation, reasonable attorneys' fees) incurred by any of them and resulting in any way from their reliance on or performance consistent with this Authorization.

_____
Signature

_____
Printed Name

_____
Date Signed

UNDER WASHINGTON LAW, TO BE VALID THIS DOCUMENT MUST BE SIGNED IN THE PRESENCE OF A WITNESS:

_____
Signature of Witness

_____
Printed Name of Witness

_____
Date Signed

WASHINGTON STATE HEALTH CARE DIRECTIVE (LIVING WILL)

1992 Revision

(According to Washington state law, a health care directive may be in the following form, but in addition may include other specific directions.)

Directive made this _____ day of _____ _____ (month, year).

I, _____, having the capacity to make health care decisions, willfully and voluntarily make known my desire that my dying shall not be artificially prolonged under the circumstances set forth below, and do hereby declare that:

(a) If at any time I should be diagnosed in writing to be in a terminal condition by the attending physician, or in a permanent unconscious condition by two physicians, and where the application of life-sustaining treatment would serve only to artificially prolong the process of my dying, I direct that such treatment be withheld or withdrawn, and that I be permitted to die naturally.

I understand by using this form that a terminal condition means an incurable and irreversible condition caused by injury, disease, or illness, that would within reasonable medical judgment cause death within a reasonable period of time in accordance with accepted medical standards, and where the application of life-sustaining treatment would serve only to prolong the process of dying.

I further understand in using this form that a permanent unconscious condition means an incurable and irreversible condition in which I am medically assessed within reasonable medical judgment as having no reasonable probability of recovery from an irreversible coma or a persistent vegetative state.

(b) In the absence of my ability to give directions regarding the use of such life-sustaining treatment, it is my intention that this directive shall be honored by my family and physician(s) as the final expression of my legal right to refuse medical or surgical treatment and I accept the consequences of such refusal. If another person is appointed to make these decisions for me, whether through a durable power of attorney or otherwise, I request that the person be guided by this directive and any other clear expressions of my desires.

_____ *I DO want to have artificially provided nutrition and hydration.*

_____ *I DO NOT want to have artificially provided nutrition and hydration.*

(d) If I have been diagnosed as pregnant and that diagnosis is known to my physician, this directive shall have no force or effect during the course of my pregnancy.

(e) I understand the full import of this directive and I am emotionally and mentally capable to make the health care decisions contained in this directive.

(f) I understand that before I sign this directive, I can add to or delete from or otherwise change the wording of this directive and that I may add to or delete from this directive at any time and that any changes shall be consistent with Washington state law or federal constitutional law to be legally valid.

(g) It is my wish that every part of this directive be fully implemented. If for any reason any part is held invalid it is my wish that the remainder of my directive be implemented.

Signed _____   _____
                                            City, County, and State of Residence

The declarer has been personally known to me, and I believe him or her to be capable of making health care decisions.

Witness _____   Witness _____

Address _____   Address _____

NOTARIZATION:

On this _____ day of _____, 19___, before me personally appeared

_____ known to be the individual described in and who executed the foregoing **Durable Power of Attorney for Health Care** and acknowledged that he/she signed said document as his/her free and voluntary act and deed for the uses and purposes therein mentioned.

IN WITNESS WHEREOF, I have hereunto set my hand and official seal this _____ day of _____, 19___.

_____
Notary Public in and for the state of Washington,

residing at _____ .

ACCEPTANCE OF APPOINTMENT:

I agree to serve as attorney-in-fact for health care decisions for _____
and agree to act in a manner consistent with his/her **Health Care Directive (Living Will)** or as otherwise communicated or expressed. I understand that this document gives me authority for health care decisions only if the declarant becomes incompetent or loses decision-making capacity, and that this authority may be revoked at any time.

_____   _____
(signature of attorney-in-fact)   (date)

_____   _____
(signature of first alternate)   (date)

_____   _____
(signature of second alternate)   (date)

DURABLE POWER OF ATTORNEY FOR HEALTH CARE

BY THIS DOCUMENT I intend to create a Durable Power of Attorney for Health Care under chapter 11.94 Revised Code of Washington.

APPOINTMENT: I, _____ , do hereby appoint

(name) _____ , (address) _____

_____ , as my attorney-in-fact for health care decisions, granting him/her the authority to consent or refuse consent to any care, treatment, or procedure to treat or maintain my physical or mental condition. This power of attorney shall become effective upon my mental incompetence or loss of decision-making capacity. If protective procedures are commenced, I nominate my attorney-in-fact as the guardian of my person.

DIRECTIONS: In exercising this authority, my attorney-in-fact shall make decisions consistent with my desires concerning use of life-sustaining procedures as stated in my **Health Care Directive** (**Living Will**) or otherwise communicated or expressed.

AUTHORITY: In the event of my loss of decision-making capacity, my attorney-in-fact shall have all the powers, discretions and rights that I would have, if competent or retaining decision-making capacity, to consent to my medical surgical or hospital care, to consent to the provision, withholding or withdrawal of life-sustaining procedures, to consent to my admission to or transfer from a health care facility, and to decide the

INDEMNITY: My attorney-in-fact shall have no personal liability for my expenses incurred or acts performed while acting in good faith under the terms of this document. I hold harmless and indemnify the attorney-in-fact from all expenses incurred on my behalf.

DURATION: This power of attorney for health care will continue in force from the date executed until revoked by my oral or written notice to my attorney-in-fact or to my physician or other health care provider.

ALTERNATES: If the person named above as my attorney-in-fact is not available, or becomes unable or unwilling to act on my behalf, or if I revoke that person's appointment as my attorney-in-fact, then I appoint the following persons to serve as my alternate attorney-in-fact to make health care decisions for me, such persons to serve in the order listed:

A. First alternate _____
    (insert name and address)

B. Second alternate _____
    (insert name and address)

SIGNATURE:
I sign my name to this **Durable Power of Attorney for Health Care**

on this _____ day of _____, 19___ at (city) _____, Washington.

_____
(signature)

The People's Memorial Society has chapters in many towns and cities across the United States and Canada. For information on the memorial society nearest you, please call or write:

FUNERAL AND MEMORIAL SOCIETIES OF
AMERICA, INC.
6900 LOST LAKE ROAD
EGG HARBOR, WISCONSIN 54209
FAX/TEL: 414-868-3168